Winston
CHURCHILL
AND HIS GREAT WARS

by Alan MacDonald
Illustrated by Clive Goddard

Hippo

Scholastic Children's Books,
Commonwealth House, 1–19 New Oxford Street,
London WC1A 1NU, UK

A division of Scholastic Ltd
London ~ New York ~ Toronto ~ Sydney ~ Auckland
Mexico City ~ New Delhi ~ Hong Kong

Published in the UK by Scholastic Ltd, 2004

ISBN 0 439 96791 0

Printed and bound by AIT Nørhaven A/S, Denmark

CONTENTS

INTRODUCTION

Winston Churchill – everybody has heard of him.

HE BECAME PRIME MINISTER!

HE STOPPED HITLER!

HE PUT UP TWO FINGERS!

Yes, Winston Churchill's dead famous for being the Prime Minister who won the Second World War and saved Britain from the Nazis. In a recent poll to find the Greatest Brit of All Time, Winston was voted number one, beating Nelson, Shakespeare, Queen Elizabeth I and loads of other big names in British history. Most people agree that Winston Churchill is the greatest leader that Britain has ever had.

Winston's winning role in the Second World War is well known, but that's only half his story. He didn't actually become Prime Minister until he was 65 years old, so what had he been doing for the rest of his life? Certainly not twiddling his thumbs!

Right from the start it was clear that Winston was cut out for greatness. He began his career as a soldier and it wasn't long before he became a hero of the Boer War. Soon after, he entered Parliament, ran the Navy during the First World War and spent time dodging shells in the trenches. When it came to telling great war stories, Churchill was the all-time champion.

And even when there wasn't a war on, Winston's life was just as colourful and surprising. Did you know he…

• Was bottom of the class at school
• Escaped from prison
• Kept a budgie which pooped on ministers' heads

• Met the President of America in the nuddy
• Could lay 60 bricks in an hour.

Winston Churchill was not only Britain's greatest leader, he was also bold, brilliant and just a teensy bit big-headed. This earned him some criticism, but luckily Winston was always funnier than his enemies. Some of his best jokes are collected in this book. You'll also discover the oddities of *Winston's World* and relive the great events of the century through the headlines in *The Winston Weekly*. And if you'd like to know Winston's private thoughts, you can read exclusive extracts from his *Lost Diary* (a book previously unknown because it was ... um, lost). So read on to find out how Winston changed the course of the 20th century. It's a story full of blood, battles and whopping big cigars...

AND IT'S ALL ABOUT **ME!**

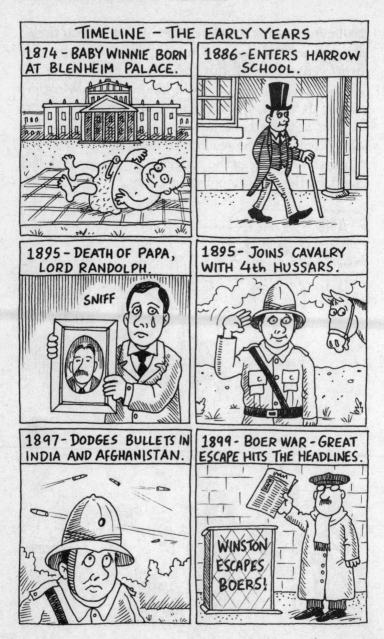

TIMELINE - THE EARLY YEARS

1874 - BABY WINNIE BORN AT BLENHEIM PALACE.

1886 - ENTERS HARROW SCHOOL.

1895 - DEATH OF PAPA, LORD RANDOLPH.

SNIFF

1895 - JOINS CAVALRY WITH 4th HUSSARS.

1897 - DODGES BULLETS IN INDIA AND AFGHANISTAN.

1899 - BOER WAR - GREAT ESCAPE HITS THE HEADLINES.

WINSTON ESCAPES BOERS!

1900 – TORY MP FOR OLDHAM.

1904 – DITCHES TORIES FOR LIBERALS.

LIBERAL PARTY →

1908 – PRESIDENT OF BOARD OF TRADE.

PREZ

1908 – MARRIES CLEMMIE HOZIER.

1910-11 – HOME SECRETARY SHOOT OUT ON SIDNEY STREET.

1911 – A NEW HAT – FIRST LORD OF THE ADMIRALTY.

WINSTON GROWS UP

Winston Churchill was a man with greatness in his blood. Throughout his life – even when he was in a battle with bullets flying all around him – Winston believed that he had a *Destiny*. In other words he reckoned he was meant to do something important and extraordinary with his life. It turned out that he was right.

Winston was marked for greatness from the start. He wasn't born in a hospital, he was born in a big palace called Blenheim in Oxfordshire. Take a look at his family and you'll see that they weren't exactly ordinary either.

FATHER –
Lord Randolph
Churchill,
rising star MP

MOTHER –
Jennie, daughter
of an American
moneybags

GRANDAD –
7th Duke of
Marlborough

BABY
WINSTON

ANCESTOR –
1st Duke of Marlborough-
great British hero

1874

Little Winston arrived in the world before anyone was expecting him. One morning in November 1874, Lady Randolph Churchill* was out walking with a shooting party at Blenheim Palace when she slipped and fell. A few days later she was riding in a pony carriage over

*In those days Ladies took their husband's names so Winston's mum was known as Lady Randolph. Daft but true.

bumpy ground, when she felt sudden pains. Winston was on his way, so eager to make his entrance that he was two months early.

He was born on 30 November 1874 and probably looked something like this.

Actually the cigar became his trademark later, but the fat cheeks and bald head would stay with him most of his life. Once, when a mother showed Winston her baby declaring that it looked just like him, he replied:

Madam, all babies look like me.

Famously forgotten

Little Winnie didn't have a happy childhood. His parents were too busy to give him much attention. His mother was a great beauty and sparkled in fashionable society. 'She shone for me like the Evening Star. I loved her dearly – but at a distance,' wrote Winston. Winston's father, a man with an impressive curly moustache and a brilliant career ahead of him, might as well have been a passing comet. Poor Winnie hardly ever saw his dad and spent his childhood trying – and failing – to please him. Lord Randolph was one of the brightest stars of his generation – clever, ambitious and a brilliant speaker. He must also have been short-sighted since he failed to notice the same qualities in his eldest son.

Little Winnie had to make do with his nurse while his parents were absent (which was pretty often). Winston's nurse was called Everest but his pet name for her was 'Woomany' and she was his dear, worried friend throughout his early life. Letters from Woomany to Winston were always full of anxious advice to *BE CAREFUL*:

Be sure you don't attempt to get into the train after it moves off, dear. I always feel uneasy about that because you stand at the Book Stall reading and forget your train.

When he was five, Winston acquired a brother, Jack, which was handy because he was soon going to need someone to play a part in his mock battles. By the age of seven Winston was already showing an interest in war. In fact he already commanded an army of 1,000 men, along with castles and flags. True, the soldiers were only made of lead, but Winston spent many happy hours drawing up his battle-lines on the nursery floor.

The first Duke of Marlborough – Winston's great ancestor – was a general in the ranks of Wellington and Cromwell, who defeated the French at the Battle of Blenheim in 1704. Since then the Churchill family line hadn't produced many heroes. Most of Winston's forebears were famous only for reckless living and running up whopping debts. He intended to change all that and make the name of Churchill great again.

Savage school

It wasn't long before Winston was torn away from his toy soldiers by a grim event – he had to go school. Worse still, school wasn't down the road from his house in London, it was a boarding school in Ascot, Surrey, which meant Winston would have to *live* there during term time. A few weeks before his eighth birthday, Winston arrived at St George's boarding school. He hated it, and who can blame him? The headmaster at St George's believed that a well-rounded education for little boys wasn't complete without a damn good flogging.

15

Flogging was common at public schools in Winston's day but St George's was savage by any standards. Winston remembered how the class were forced to witness each offender's punishment and 'sat quaking listening to their screams.' By the time the last blow was struck the poor boy's bottom was often a mass of blood. (And you thought *your* school was strict!)

It's hardly surprising that young Winnie made no progress whatsoever at St George's. He spent his days praying for the holidays when he could escape the threat of the cane and go home. Lady Randolph was disappointed with her son's lack of progress but, never mind, the headmaster assured her that next term they would be *more strict* with him!

Winston's school reports gave little hint of future greatness. An early report might have looked something like this.

SCHOOL REPORT	
Pupil: *Winston Churchill*	
Age: 8	
HISTORY:	*Feeble*
GEOGRAPHY:	*Feeble*
LATIN:	*Feeblus Maximus*
COMPOSITION:	*Needs to be made of sterner stuff*
WRITING:	*Slow ... as ... a ... snail*
SPELLING:	*About as dredful as can be*
EFFORT:	*Doesn't understand the meaning of hard work. Look it up.*
DISCIPLINE:	*20 of the best*
Position in class:	*13th*
Number in class:	*13*

17

Not only bottom of the class, Winston was late for lessons 20 times – and that was just in one term. His report card said: 'He is a constant trouble to everybody and is always in some scrape or other.'

St George's believed that the best way to correct a troublesome boy was to beat the trouble out of him, but Winston didn't respond well to the birch. Once he was given a flogging for stealing sugar from the pantry in the kitchens. Later he slipped into the head's room and stole his sacred straw hat from the door. Winston then took great pleasure in kicking it to pieces. This daring act of rebellion would become a legend at St George's.

HOW'S THAT FOR A HAT-TRICK?

It was Winston's poor health that came to his rescue. He was always a delicate child and suffered from mumps and measles. In September 1884 the family doctor suggested that the boy transfer to a school in Brighton where the sea air might do him good. The new boarding school was run by two sisters – the Misses Thomson – and luckily flogging wasn't on the timetable.

While at Brighton, Winston got into one of his many scrapes – but in this case the result could have been fatal.

No doubt one of the Misses Thomson would have written a letter to his mother, explaining what had happened:

> Dear Lady Churchill,
>
> I am sorry to have to tell you of an incident involving your son, Winston. Yesterday he was at work on a drawing examination when a dispute arose between him and the boy sitting next to him. It seems their tutor had lent them a knife to use in their artwork and this led to an argument.
>
> There's really no need for alarm but during the fight your son received a minor stab wound in the chest. The doctor assures me that the penknife only went in about a quarter of an inch. Winston tells me he was entirely blameless and only took hold of the boy's ear to get his attention. The other boy will be sent away as I can't say I approve of knife attacks. When children are trying to sit exams they are such a distraction.
>
> Humbly yours
> Miss Charlotte Thomson

The sinking of Lord Randolph

Winston's poor health continued in Brighton. When he was 12 he caught double pneumonia and his life was in such grave danger that both his parents actually came to visit. (As a rule they were far too busy with their important lives to waste time visiting their son.)

Young Winston pulled through but in December 1886 a different kind of disaster struck his family. The previous summer his famous Papa had been re-elected to Parliament and offered the plum job of Chancellor of the Exchequer – second only in rank to the Prime Minister and keeper of the country's piggy bank. However Lord Randolph's success was short-lived. He quarrelled with two powerful government ministers who were unwilling to make the cutbacks in spending he wanted. Randolph wasn't a man to accept defeat when he thought he was right (which, let's face it, was all the time). As a warning shot, Randolph threatened to resign if he didn't get his way. But the Prime Minister called his bluff and immediately accepted his letter of resignation.

Poor Randolph's brilliant career was over almost before it had started. Blink and you would have missed it. While he kept his seat as an MP in Parliament, he would never again be asked to sit on the top table of government.

HOW TO BE A BIG SUCCESS – BY LORD RANDOLPH

TAKE MY ADVICE, SON ... GET YOURSELF ELECTED TO PARLIAMENT. SEE THE WORLD – SECRETARY OF STATE FOR INDIA IS A GOOD START.

GET PROMOTED. AIM FOR THE TOP, BOY – NEXT STOP PRIME MINISTER.

Hooray for Harrow!

By April 1888 though, things were looking up for 13-year-old Winston. He was at a new school – Harrow. With its own swimming pool, gym and carpentry shop, Harrow was a top-drawer school for the sons of the rich and famous. Winston only scraped through the entrance exam and was happy to go there, especially as it was near London so his parents could come and visit often! (Fat chance of that.)

Children at Harrow didn't wear blazers or shirts, they dressed like dapper young gentlemen. This suited Winston, as all his life he had a passion for hats.

At Harrow, Winston was no longer bottom of the class. Later in life he liked to pretend he was a complete duffer at school but in fact Winston won prizes for history and reciting Shakespeare off by heart. Yet he was still a troublesome boy. Forgetful, careless, late for lessons and always losing his books and papers, his teachers were at their wits' end with him. Even when he was in trouble, Winston didn't know how to keep quiet.

Winston's letters home are full of desperate pleas for his mother and father to come and visit him. Lord Randolph didn't come for the entire first term but in his place sent his son a new bike. A delighted Winston rode eight miles on it. Not long afterwards he fell off and was in bed for a week with concussion. Even then, neither of his parents could spare the time to visit and he had to make do with his loyal Nurse Everest. None of the other boys would have been seen dead with their nannies, but Winston was proud as punch to walk his dear old nurse down Harrow high street in front of his classmates.

School for soldiers

One of the odd ideas at Harrow was that the boys should be trained as army cadets. This involved marches, drills and wearing military uniform. Sometimes there were even mock battles against other schools. The boys were issued with rifles and Winston's job in his first battle was to carry 100 rounds of ammunition to give away in the thick of the fight. 'It was most exciting, you could see through the smoke the enemy getting nearer and nearer,' he wrote to his parents. He didn't mention it but we assume the bullets were only blanks...

Winston had been at Harrow for over a year when his papa finally honoured him with a visit. The occasion was Speech Day and Randolph made a decision that would affect his son's entire future. Winston was to join the Army Class. Boys in the class were being prepared to enter the Army – to become officers naturally. It meant that Winston wouldn't get the chance of going to university, even though his marks were up to scratch. He had no say in his own future and his father seems to have made up his mind based on a conversation he'd had with his son years before. Once, during a holiday, Randolph found his son with 1,500 toy soldiers laid out in formations of attack. He spent 20 minutes inspecting the scene and finally asked him if he would like to go into the

Army. Winston innocently replied that he thought it would be splendid to command an army – and that was that.

For years Winston wondered if his father had recognized the qualities of a young Napoleon in him. The sad truth was that Randolph thought his oldest son too *dim* to follow a career in law or politics. That only left the Army.

Winston found the Army Class 'rather a bore', but he did show a talent for ordering other children about which would come in handy later on. One of his letters home to his mother was dictated to a classmate.

MILBANKE IS WRITING THIS FOR ME AS I AM HAVING A BATH.

(Later, many letters would be dictated to his secretaries while Winston soaked in the tub.)

Other boys at Harrow remembered Winston as a magnetic character. He 'dominated great numbers around him, many of whom were his superiors in age and prowess,' said one. This was Winston's great talent, which his father failed to recognize. If he wasn't the brainiest boy in class, he was certainly the most commanding. Even as a schoolboy Winston was a natural leader.

> *If I had two lives I would be a soldier and a politician. But as there will be no war in my time, I shall have to be a politician.*

He was right about going into politics, but wrong about war. In fact he'd get a chance to play a major role in *two* world wars. What more could a boy ask for?

The Battle of Banstead

The New Year holidays of 1891 were spent at Banstead, a house near Newmarket which Lord Randolph had rented. Lord and Lady Churchill were away, of course, but 16-year-old Winston had his brother Jack and his two small cousins to keep him company. He lost no time in recruiting them into his private army. You can read about these early skirmishes in his Lost Diary…

WINSTON'S LOST DIARY

January 4 1891

Hoorah! The Den is finished. We worked like slaves all day - at least the others did while I issued orders and told them where to dig. It is a fine castle made from mud and planks with a straw floor. Our fortress is defended by a ditch which serves as a capital moat. Any intruders will be repelled by fierce cannon-fire (apples from my home-made catapult - the rotten ones explode impressively!)

I am commander in chief - naturally - and Jack is my loyal lieutenant.

Sometimes I let my little cousins Shane and Hugh join our army and I drill them in marching and presenting arms. (Shane will burst into tears which I've told him is a disgrace in a soldier.) Sometimes they are the enemy and must lay siege to our fortress. Then the cannons fire, the apples fly and the smoke of battle fills the air!

Back at Harrow after the holidays, Winston got into another row. While he was out walking with four other boys they came across a disused factory. The building was a ruin with most of the windows broken, although a few still remained intact. To Winston and his pals it was an irresistible target and a few well-aimed stones struck home. Unfortunately a watchman witnessed the target practice and complained to the Head of Harrow. Winston and his pals got 'swished' – which gave the headmaster some target practice of his own.

Pounds, shillings and debts

Winston's parents were less annoyed about the caning than their son's careless habit of running up huge debts. Winston's letters home were full of requests for more money. In one week he spent 15 shillings, which in those days was almost enough to keep a poor family of six or seven people. Try as he might, Winston couldn't help living beyond his means, a failing that would continue for the rest of his life.

WINSTON'S LOST DIARY

March 10 1891

Income this week: 10 shillings

Expenses this week: 11 shillings

Am stony broke. Shall have to consider selling bicycle. Then what about buying that splendid bulldog that's so friendly? After all, Papa kept a bulldog at Eton, it's only fair I should have one.

Awful exams

The following year, Winston's schooldays were coming to an end and the dreaded Army Exam was looming. Winston knew the exam would be tough and worked hard, sometimes studying for ten hours a day. In between his books he found time to enter – and win – the public-school fencing championship. Writing home, he was typically modest about his triumph.

Winston took the Army Exam in the summer of 1892 – while his father and the Conservatives were losing the General Election to the Liberals. Winston wasn't sure he wanted to go into the Army, but his father was still set on the idea. The plan was for Winston to go to Sandhurst, the top-notch college for officers. However his exam results let him down and he failed to get in.

In November he took the exam a second time – and failed once again.

In despair, his parents sent him away to Captain James's 'crammer' school. A crammer is just what the name suggests, it aims to cram as many facts into your head as possible in a short time. It was 18-year-old Winston's final shot at the Army. If he had failed a third time his father would probably have put him into the business world and maybe his life would have turned out as dull as a bank statement. Luckily it didn't come to that.

His teachers at the crammer school complained he was more inclined to teach them than to learn from them.

Nevertheless when the results came it was third time lucky. Winston had got into the Army – not into the infantry as planned, but he had made the cavalry (which didn't have quite such high standards). Winston was relieved and delighted and sent telegrams to his family to tell them of his great triumph. His grandma was overjoyed and promised he would get a charger to ride. Lord Randolph, however, was not impressed. Imagine how poor Winston must have felt when he got the following letter:

There are two ways of winning in an examination, one creditable the other the reverse.

With all the advantages you had, with all the abilities which you foolishly think yourself to possess... with all the efforts that have been made to make your life easy & agreeable ... this is the grand result that you come up among the 2nd rate and 3rd rate class who are only good for commissions in a cavalry regiment!

REAL LETTER EXTRACT

Winston had joined the Army Class to please his father, he had accepted a career in the Army and taken the exam to please his father. Having passed he had a right to expect a little praise, but instead he was told he was a third-rate failure. You can imagine how crushed he must have felt. Lord Randolph had always been stern and demanding, but even Winston must have been taken aback. What he didn't know was that his father was seriously ill and beginning to lose his marbles. Within two years, Randolph would be dead.

As for Winston, the Army and the world beyond beckoned with the chance to finally make his mark. It wouldn't be long before he attracted the world's attention.

WINSTON AT A GALLOP

Winston arrived at the Royal Military College at Sandhurst in September 1893, where he was to spend 18 months. The discipline was strict and made Harrow look like a teddy bears' picnic. No excuse was ever accepted – if you didn't know something, that was your own stupid fault and you got punished anyway. Winston's famous lateness and untidiness would not be tolerated. After a short while he decided he was going to enjoy it.

WINSTON'S LOST DIARY
Sandhurst, November 1893
Monday – Learnt all sorts of
complicated knots. Jolly useful for
lashing big pieces of wood together
which I expect comes in handy in the
middle of a battle.

Tuesday - Have been learning to make sketch maps. The officer in charge said mine was excellent though not really necessary to draw every cow in the field.

Wednesday - Shooting practice. Am becoming a pretty good shot with both a rifle and revolver.

Friday - Riding class. Eight hours in the saddle followed by a game of polo. My bottom hasn't been so sore since I was last flogged at Harrow.

Saturday - Ho hum! Weekends are so dull with nothing to shoot at and no one to order you about.

Going, going, gone

In 1895, just before Winston finished at Sandhurst, his father died. Lord Randolph had been ill for some time and his mind had become increasingly feeble and wandering. It was hard for Winston to see the man who had made brilliant speeches in Parliament, confused and slurring his words. Winston had never succeeded in getting close to his father. During his whole life they'd only shared three or four long conversations. Once, when Winston suggested that he might help with some of his father's letters, the icy look Randolph gave his son froze him to stone. Lord Randolph died three weeks before he was 46. He left behind a wife saddled with debts and an older son determined to show that his father had been wrong about him.

The dashing hussar

Four weeks after his father's death, Winston joined the cavalry as a second lieutenant with the 4th Hussars. A cavalry officer looks rather silly without a horse and Winston was lucky that his was paid for by his grandma, Duchess Lily. He also got a dashing uniform. However Winston wasn't content to shine his buttons, he wanted to be in the thick of a war. His broad plan for the future ran like this:

1 Fight in as many battles as possible
2 Win a stack of medals
3 Make myself famous
4 Leave Army, enter politics and become a famous MP like Papa

Winston never saw himself as a career soldier, he was only in it for the fame and glory.

His first posting was to India and things started badly. When his boat landed at Bombay, Winston hurt himself trying to disembark in rough waters. Grabbing hold of an iron ring on the dock, the boat pitched in the waves, wrenching his shoulder badly. 'I scrambled up all right, made a few remarks of a general character … hugged my shoulder and thought no more about it,' he wrote in a letter home. Unfortunately he had dislocated his shoulder and for the rest of his life it would 'pop out' at unfortunate moments. He was forced to give up tennis and had to play polo with one arm strapped to his side (fortunately not the one holding the polo stick!).

India proved unexciting to begin with – 'a godless land of snobs and bores,' thought Winston, who was obviously mixing with the British. Luckily there would be plenty of excitement before long. Meanwhile Churchill shared a pink-and-white bungalow with two fellow officers. Army life wasn't exactly what Winston was hoping for, as his letters home probably betrayed.

Dear Mama,
Life out here is stupid and dull but I'm making myself as comfortable as possible. I have a butler, a Dressing Boy and a groom to look after my horse. We breakfast early and have to be on parade by six am. Then it's a bath, another breakfast to eat and nothing to do all day but sleep, read the papers or write. At four o'clock we practice polo. All very tiresome with nobody to shoot at all. Please send me my card table, bicycle, books to read and a butterfly-collecting kit.
Your worn-out son *Winston*

HOBBIES WITH WINSTON: POLO

Books and polo were Winston's two great loves during the long, hot days in India. He tried to make up for his lack of a university education by reading fat volumes of history and politics. When he took to the polo field he played in typical Winston fashion. One observer recalled: 'He rides in the game like heavy cavalry getting into position for the assault. He charges in, neither deft nor graceful, but full of tearing physical energy… He bears down opposition by the weight of his dash and strikes the ball. Did I say strikes? He slashes the ball.'

HOW TO PLAY POLO — 1. POLO IS PLAYED BY TWO OPPOSING TEAMS ON HORSEBACK.

2. PLAYERS STRIKE THE BALL WITH A POLO STICK AND TRY TO SCORE GOALS.

WHACK!

3. THE GAME LASTS AN HOUR AND IS DIVIDED INTO 'CHUKKAS' OF SEVEN AND A HALF MINUTES.

1st Chukka

Winston's polo team – the 4th Hussars – took their polo pretty seriously. Arriving in Bombay, they bought 25 well-trained polo ponies to give them an advantage over their rivals. The height of their success came in November 1896 at a tournament in Hyderabad, 700 miles away. On this occasion the prize at stake was a silver cup worth 1,000 rupees. When Winston played in the final match a huge crowd of eight or nine thousand Indians turned out to watch. Winston's team came up against the local team of 'turbaned warriors' whose every stroke and goal was cheered wildly by their supporters. They were a little disappointed when Winston's Hussars won the cup.

Later in life as an MP Winston would take the field for the House of Commons team against the Guards.

No hour of life is lost that is spent in the saddle.

Into action

Young Winston was eager to get on and he couldn't do that lazing around and playing polo. When a revolt against the British broke out on the Indian frontier in 1897, he got his mother to pull some strings so that he could be sent straight to the fighting. Initially he went out as a war reporter writing letters for the *Daily Telegraph*. But that was just a means of getting to the action. Winston generally found journalism and soldiering could be combined pretty effectively. He could make money from one and grab the glory with the other. If there was fighting anywhere, he would be found in the thick of it.

The British commander – the aptly named General Bindon Blood – was easily persuaded to accept Winston as an officer (he would write his reports for the *Telegraph* in his time off). The fighting would be fierce – the Afghan rebels had a nasty reputation for making chopped liver of any enemy soldiers who fell into their hands. Yet Winston didn't mind the risks, he believed in his destiny.

> I have faith in my star —
> that I am intended to do
> something in this world.

His first day in action was 16 September and it would surely have filled at least a page in his diary.

WINSTON'S LOST DIARY
September 16 1897

What a day! The most glorious of my life so far!

We rode forward with 1,300 cavalry to meet the enemy near the frontier. I rode my grey pony all along the skirmish line when everyone else was lying down to take cover. Crazy maybe, but nothing is too daring for me when I've got an audience.

The enemy drove us back and we retreated under fire. The bullets were whistling past and the dust kicking up all around me. Thrilling!

Things really hotted up when the enemy came within 40 yards of us. I was forced to fire my revolver nine times in self defence and to grab a rifle from a wounded man and fire off 40 rounds. All together I was under fire for 13 hours without cease.
With any luck tomorrow will be just as good.

BANG
BANG

Winston received the first of many medals for his coolness under fire. At school he had felt like a coward. He was small and (apart from fencing) didn't excel at sport. Yet when it came to staring death in the face all fear seemed to desert him. Winston desired a reputation for personal bravery and would take any wild risk to get himself noticed. He turned his adventures in India into a book, a personal account of the war. In the future he would write many books on many wars, but always with the same hero.

HOW I WON THE WAR
WS Churchill

By 1898 Winston was fighting in the Sudan, at the Battle of Omdurman, where he was part of one of the last cavalry charges in British history.

As if that wasn't enough, Winston was soon heading for South Africa and the Boer War. As it turned out, it wasn't a bore at all, the war would make Winston Churchill a household name.

The glory train

In October 1899, Winston was on his way to Cape Town in South Africa to involve himself in another war. Again he got himself sent out as a reporter – this time writing for the *Morning Post*. The Boer War was fought to prevent the spread of the British Empire in Africa. The rebels were South African farmers – known as Boers – who resented their land being added to Queen Victoria's private collection.

Naturally the *Morning Post* didn't expect their reporter to take part in the fighting and naturally Winston was hoping to do just that. Shortly after his arrival he headed straight for trouble. He boarded an armoured train bound for the area where the Boers were laying siege to the British town of Ladysmith. Somewhere out in no-man's land, the train ran into a Boer ambush and was derailed. Caught under heavy fire, Winston should have kept his head down like any sensible reporter. Instead, being a reckless daredevil, he tried to organize an escape. Two of the derailed trucks were lying across the line, blocking the engine's way. Under a hail of bullets and exploding shells, Winston tried to move the trucks. At one point the engine driver received a wound to the head and told Churchill, 'I'm finished.'

'Buck up a bit and I will stick to you,' replied Winston coolly. Using the engine as a battering ram, they managed to knock the trucks off the line. Then Winston got all the wounded onto the engine and it pulled away out of danger.

Most people would have felt they'd done enough. Not Winston. He got off the train and *walked back* to try and help the 50 British soldiers who were still carrying on the fight against the ambush. This turned out to be a bad move – the soldiers had surrendered and Winston found himself looking down the barrel of a rifle. He was a prisoner of the Boers.

The great escape

When the survivors of the ambush got back to base, the story of the young reporter's heroism soon spread. Many of the newspapers suggested Winston should receive the top gong for bravery – the Victoria Cross – if he ever got out of prison. Needless to say, Winston was already planning a swift exit. At first he tried to persuade the Boers that he was only a harmless reporter. Having witnessed his part in the battle for the train, they weren't falling for that one. In their view he was a dangerous prisoner of war. Churchill found himself spending his 25th birthday in jail.

But just two weeks later he made his escape. Winston's plan was to make a break with two other prisoners called Captain Haldane and Sergeant Major Brockie. When the guard was lighting his pipe, Winston took his chance to scramble over the prison wall from the cover of a toilet. His companions weren't so lucky. Haldane was seen by the sentry who levelled his rifle at him. With Brockie, he decided escape was too risky.

Outside the wall, Winston waited half an hour and eventually decided he was on his own. Ahead lay what seemed an impossible journey. He had 300 miles to travel across enemy territory with no map or compass to guide him. He didn't speak a word of Dutch and in his pocket he had nothing but £75 in British notes and a few pieces of chocolate. It was to be a hair-raising journey but Winston would have a great adventure story to tell for years to come.

Winston's escape had taken nine days. The story hit the headlines all over South Africa and back home in Britain. While he was on the road many rumours went round – one said he'd been arrested, another that he was disguised as a Catholic priest. In fact four different men were arrested on suspicion of being Winston Churchill. He was a wanted man and the Boers wanted him so badly they issued posters with a less-than-flattering description of him:

WANTED DEAD OR ALIVE
WINSTON CHURCHILL
Escaped prisoner, 25 years old
About 5 foot 8 inches tall
Walks with a slight stoop,
pale appearance,
almost invisible small moustache,
speaks through the nose,
cannot pronounce the letter 'S'.
Last seen in a brown suit of clothes.
£25 REWARD

Admittedly not everyone was a fan. Captain Haldane grumbled that Winston's version of the story failed to mention that he'd left his two fellow prisoners in the lurch. (Months later they followed, tunnelling their way out of the Boer prison.) Winston replied that he *had* waited, expecting them to join him. When they didn't appear he had no choice but to go on alone. What else could he do? Either way, the story caused a sensation and Winston was proclaimed a hero. The British had just suffered a series of humiliating defeats against the Boers and the tale of young Churchill's heroic derring-do was just what they wanted to hear. Overnight the young reporter became a celebrity. Everyone wanted to sing his praises – though none louder than Winston himself. He wrote up his story in articles for the *Morning Post* and later turned it into a book of his South African adventures. By the age of 25, Churchill would boast, he had written as many books as Moses (five).

Winston stayed on as a soldier and reporter to the end of the war. At times he seemed to lead a charmed life. On one occasion the feather in his hat was cut through by a bullet, while Winston escaped unharmed. Maybe it was just as well that his soldiering days were over and he was about to turn to Parliament.

VOTE FOR WINSTON!

On 10 July 1900 a sketch of 25-year-old Winston Churchill appeared in the popular magazine *Vanity Fair* along with the following description:

He is a clever fellow who has the courage of his opinions… He can write and he can fight… He is something of a sportsman; who prides himself on being practical rather than a dandy; he is ambitious; he means to get on and he loves his country. But he can hardly be a slave of any Party.

Most of this was true and the last part would prove especially accurate. Winston joined the Conservative Party to stand for Parliament, but he was always a loose cannon likely to go off in any direction. What he thought, he spoke, even if that meant ruffling a few feathers and making him unpopular with his party. In the future he would even be prepared to swap political parties (twice).

However in 1900, the Conservatives welcomed him with open arms. He was a war hero, and great crowds flocked to hear his speeches. In the coming general election Winston was just the man for the job.

Politics are almost as exciting as war and quite as dangerous.

When Winston arrived in Oldham, where he was standing for Parliament, a vast crowd of 10,000 people turned out to meet him. (Today most politicians are grateful if they can draw three people and a dog!) There were flags and drums and people cheered themselves hoarse for two hours. Winston didn't need any persuasion to tell them the tale of his great escape and cleverly dropped in the name of the Oldham engineer, Mr Dewsnip, who had helped him hide in the South African coal mine.

The shpeech maker

During the General Election of 1900 Winston was in demand as a speaker all over the country. Soon he would be making speeches in the House of Commons, and during the Second World War many of his words would claim a place in history. It's all the more surprising then that Churchill had trouble with public speaking. Some have claimed that Churchill had a stutter. This isn't true. His problem lay in pronouncing the letter 'S' which came out as a 'Sh' sound. (Funnily enough his father had the same shpeech defect.)

Lord Rosebery advised him to take elocution (speech) lessons but Churchill feared that he would never master his difficulty. (He was right.) One of his early girlfriends, Muriel Wilson, remembered Winston walking up and down the drive of her parents' home reciting the lines:

A favourite mannerism of Churchill's was to stand with his hands on his hips and beam with satisfaction when he'd just made a point in a speech. At other times when he got excited – which was often – he seemed to be punching home his words with both hands in the air like an enthusiastic football fan. Sometimes his speeches were interrupted by hecklers in the crowd but Winston was never at a loss for a witty reply.

The election of October 1900 saw Winston come second. It looked like he'd lost again and *The Times* reported his failure. In fact he'd won, since a large city like Oldham could elect not one, but two members for Parliament. At the youthful age of 25, Winston had achieved his ambition of entering Parliament like his famous papa. He promptly set off on a speaking tour of the country. Before long the Conservatives had been re-elected to government.

WINSTON'S WORLD: POLITICS

In the 1900s the two great political parties were the Conservatives and the Liberals. The Labour Party was just a troublesome infant with only two MPs.

Conservatives and Liberals were difficult to tell apart in Parliament as they both wore top hats (unlike Keir Hardie, the Labour MP who shockingly turned up in a cloth cap).

Conservatives were known as Tories while Liberals included Whigs – though sadly they no longer wore any. Winston had joined the Conservatives because it was his father's party and his natural home. But he wasn't a tame MP who always stuck by his party. He belonged to a young and rebellious group of Tories known as Hughligans.

Hooligans in the 1900s were rather more polite than they are today. Winston's pals were more likely to take tea and moan about the state of the country than start fights at football matches. The name 'Hughligans' in fact came from their leader, Lord

Hugh Cecil. One of the issues bothering them was Tariff Reform. In fact it bothered Winston so much that it led him to swap teams, changing from the Conservative Party to the Liberals.

Crossing the floor

Winston's decision in May 1904 to leave the Conservatives wasn't popular, to say the least. Crossing to the opposite political party was thought shocking behaviour, rather like showing your knees in public. MPs were supposed to be loyal to their party, whether the party was right or wrong. As far as the Tories were concerned, Winston was a two-faced traitor and it would take another 20 years before they were ready to forgive him.

Yet to Winston the matter was simple. It was a matter of right and wrong – he was right and his party was wrong. His decision was probably helped by the fact that he was leaving a dead-end party to join a party with a future. The Liberals were about to become the new government and Winston aimed to be part of it. For the next ten years his career was on the rise. He started out as the tedious-sounding Under Secretary for the Colonies but by the start of the First World War he would be running the entire British Navy.

The marrying kind

Meanwhile Winston's life was changing in other ways. He was in love. To tell the truth, Winston had been in love before and had even got as far as proposing marriage more than once.

You could say that when Clementine Hozier came along she was Winston's fourth choice. That would be unfair though – when Winnie met Clemmie he'd finally found his soul mate. The marriage would form the bedrock of his life, lasting more than 56 years, until his death.

Clementine herself was from a titled family like Winston's – she was the granddaughter of the Scottish Earl of Airlie. Sadly her family didn't have any Scots castles to boast of and she had to wash and iron her own party dresses. Winston and Clemmie first met at a dance in 1904. On this occasion Winston didn't ask her to dance, he just stood and stared. Clemmie thought him stuck-up and rude. But four years later they met again at a dinner party and things were quite different. Winston's diary would have recorded the whirlwind romance:

WINSTON'S LOST DIARY
March 1908

Sat next to the most enchanting girl at dinner. Her name is Clementine. She has blue-green eyes, an elegant nose and looks like a Greek goddess. Gave her my fullest attention at dinner. Ignored Lady Lusard, sitting on my left who looks more like a Greek ruin. 'Have you read my book about my father?' I asked Clementine. 'No,' she replied. No? I thought everyone had read it!!! Will send her a copy so I'll have a good excuse to go and ask for it back.

July 20
Have been seeing a lot of Clemmie and
she is enchanting. In fact I want to
marry her. Will invite her to stay at
Grandad's palace in Blenheim. Could
there be anywhere more romantic to
pop the question?

August 11, Blenheim Palace
Still have not plucked up the courage to
ask her. Am so stupid and clumsy with
women when usually I'm so charming
and irresistible. Tomorrow could be my
last chance before she goes home.

August 12
Just back from a walk with Clemmie.
The heavens opened and the rain came
down in buckets. What luck! Sheltered
in the Temple of Diana and even I
couldn't bungle such a chance. Proposed
and she accepted! The
happiest day of my life!
Must go and dry my socks.

Clemmie was in many ways Winston's perfect match. Not only attractive, she was serious and intelligent. She might have gone on to university but in those days girls were expected to find husbands, not study French or History.

Clementine was only 23, ten years younger than Winston when they married in September 1908. Their marriage would prove a great success. Clemmie's chief concern was Winston and his chief concern was himself. Winston wrote that they got married and 'lived happily ever after', but he was never an easy person to live with. Clemmie would have to put up with his extravagant spending, his drinking and gambling, not to mention his part in two world wars.

Clemmie's affectionate nickname for him was 'Pig' and he called her 'Kat' or 'Cat'. Their love would ride out all the storms to come.

Stormy seas

When Winston married Clementine, Britain was entering a stormy period. Two major forces in society were beating on the government's door to demand attention. One was the women's suffragette movement, the other was the working classes who were equally fed up with being ignored. In Ireland there was bitter opposition to Home Rule while abroad the clouds were gathering with the threat of Germany. In one way or another Winston Churchill was involved in all of these problems. At school he had been a troublesome boy, in politics he was no different. Winston didn't have to go looking for trouble, it followed him around like a dog.

WINSTON'S WORLD: VOTES FOR WOMEN

In 1912 seven million men had the right to vote but not one single woman. It depended on owning property which meant that only well-off males qualified. Women in Edwardian society were supposed to leave important matters to men. A woman's place was in the home where she looked after the children and gave orders to the servants if she had any.

But not all women were content with this state of affairs; in fact some of them were hopping mad. Women who campaigned for the vote were known as suffragettes. Many suffragettes got fed up with the government ignoring their demands for equality. They decided actions spoke louder than words. They chained themselves to railings, broke windows and went on hunger strike in prison. In 1909 a policy of force-feeding was introduced. Hunger strikers were pinned down by warders while milk was fed to them through a tube stuck up their nose.

When the Liberals won the 1910 election, Churchill continued the unpopular policy of force-feeding as Home Office Minister. Once he was attacked outside Bristol station by a suffragette with a dog whip, crying, 'Take that in the name of the insulted women of England.' Another time a protester almost pushed him under a train and he was only saved by Clementine's quick action.

Like most men of his time, Churchill had a blind spot on the issue of women's votes. Sympathetic at first, he became stubborn when anyone tried to browbeat him.

I AM NOT GOING TO BE HENPECKED INTO A QUESTION OF SUCH IMPORTANCE.

CLONK!

Trigger-happy Churchill

While the suffragettes were rebelling, the workers were revolting. In 1910 the miners went on strike. Things got out of hand in the Rhondda Valley in South Wales where miners in the town of Tonypandy rioted in the streets and smashed shop windows. Something had to be done and Winston as Home Office Minister was in the hot seat.

The local police constable called for the troops to be sent in which risked pouring oil on the flames (in Queen Victoria's famous phrase). If angry miners and troops came face to face, someone was certainly going to get hurt.

Winston allowed only 400 soldiers to go and instead swelled the ranks of the local police with Metropolitan police from London. In the event the riots were brought under control with the police beating off the strikers using rolled-up mackintoshes.

Elsewhere things got more serious, two strikers were killed and soldiers made them retreat by fixing bayonets.

For years to come Winston would be tarnished with the claim that he used troops to put down the strike. The cry of 'Tonypandy' was often used against him at public meetings. In fact Churchill's sympathy was with the strikers and he wanted their cause to be taken seriously. 'The strikers are very poor, miserably paid and now nearly starving,' he said.

The accusation that Winston was 'trigger happy' was brought up again in an incident known as the Battle of Sidney Street. It's a typical example of how Churchill was drawn to trouble like a magnet. Most government ministers stayed at their desks and left dangerous jobs to the police or the Army. Not Winston. If there was a battle to be fought on the streets, he grabbed his top hat and got down there at the double.

The papers next day went to town reporting the sensational drama and Winston's starring role.

⋘ THE WINSTON WEEKLY ⋙
4 January 1911

CHURCHILL IN DEADLY STREET DRAMA

Man of action Winston Churchill was at it again yesterday. When dangerous killers occupied a house on Sidney Street, the Minister hot-footed it there to direct the siege personally.

The drama began to unfold late last night when three men – including 'Peter the Painter' – a known Russian anarchist – burgled a house in London's East End. Three policemen who tried to arrest them were shot

and the murderers were tracked to a house in Sidney Street.

PETER THE PAINTER

When Mr Churchill arrived on the scene shortly before midday, the police were bolstered by 20 Scots Guards, armed with rifles while the criminals were firing from every window.

Under Fire

While bullets zipped off the brickwork, Churchill was seen

crouching behind a wall directing the attack. Minutes later the besieged house caught fire. The fire brigade were prevented from taking any action on Churchill's orders. 'I thought it better to let the house burn down rather than spend good British lives in rescuing those ferocious rascals,' said Mr Churchill afterwards. Two charred bodies were found in the destroyed house, but not that of the mysterious Russian.

Fire Brigade fiddled while house burned.

Not everyone was impressed by Churchill's eagerness to put himself in the firing line.

The Conservatives took great pleasure in mocking the Minister's habit of deserting his desk and looking for trouble. In Parliament, Arthur Balfour remarked, to howls of laughter, 'He (Winston) and a photographer were both risking valuable lives. I understand what the photographer was doing, but what was the honourable gentlemen doing?'

To be fair to Winston he hadn't actually been directing the siege. He'd left that to the police but backed their authority. The only order he'd given was to a policeman standing right behind him. Winston told him to be careful where he was pointing his 12-bore shotgun!

Film of the dramatic siege was shown in London cinemas for nights afterwards and when Winston was shown the reaction wasn't enthusiastic.

Try as he might, Winston could never be an ordinary humdrum politician and public feeling was divided. You either loved or hated Winston but you certainly couldn't ignore him. Nancy Astor, who, in 1919, became the first woman to enter Parliament, constantly argued with Churchill but rarely got the better of him.

WINSTON AT WAR

In 1911, to his great delight, Winston found himself a new hat to wear.

With Germany and Austria-Hungary building up their armies, the clouds of war were gathering. Churchill was appointed First Lord of the Admiralty. Britain was in a race with Germany to build the strongest navy in the world and someone was needed to speed things up. Who better than Winston Churchill, the young minister who approached everything with the energy of ten men?

Winston launched himself into the task with enthusiasm. Before he was at the Admiralty he'd argued strongly against wasting money on defence. Now he was all in favour of building new warships whatever the cost. Britannia's security depended on its ability to rule the waves, he argued.

The warring admirals

The Navy that Churchill inherited was hopelessly divided. For years two admirals – 'Jackie' Fisher and Lord Charles Beresford – had been fighting their own private war with each other. Both admirals had their own supporters who hated each other. The result was stagnation since nothing could ever be agreed upon. Churchill arrived when the warring admirals had reluctantly retired (although Fisher was far from finished.) He swept through the Navy like a force-ten gale. He improved the conditions of the sailors and introduced the Royal Naval Air Force. Instead of sitting in a comfortable Whitehall office, he often installed himself on the Admiralty yacht *Enchantress* and spent eight months afloat in the three years before war broke out. No detail was too small for the new First Lord of the Admiralty, he poked his nose into everything. It was true he could also be rude and insulting. On one occasion he told off a high-ranking admiral for not presenting his report in better English. Nevertheless by 1913 Churchill had done what he set out to do – the British Navy was ready for war.

...AND YOUR PUNCTUATION ISN'T VERY GOOD EITHER!

HOBBIES WITH WINSTON: FLYING LESSONS

Winston always felt that the best way to understand something was to try it yourself. Flying was one example. You might think flying had got little to do with the Navy, but Winston had been building a naval air force, and he felt it was essential that he should learn to fly.

In 1913 flying was a risky business. Planes were still in their infancy and going up in one was about as safe as taking a cabin on the *Titanic*. It didn't stop Winston taking flying lessons to the great dismay of Clemmie who begged him to stop before he went and killed himself. Winston's letters home reveal he eventually had a change of heart – but only after he'd been up in the air 140 times!

6 June 1914

I will not fly any more...

This is a wrench because I was on the verge of taking my pilot's certificate... But I must admit the numerous fatalities this year would justify you in complaining if I continue to share the risks - as I am proud to do - of these good fellows. I am sure my nerve, my spirits and my virtue were improved by it. But at your expense, my poor pussy cat! I am so sorry.

REAL LETTER EXTRACT

Countdown to war

Across the North Sea, Germany had been keeping a watchful eye on the enlarging of Britain's Navy. Every ship that Churchill built was matched by his opposite number, Von Tirpitz, for the German Navy. The situation in Europe was finely balanced – with all the major powers afraid of their rivals growing any stronger. One spark could result in war. On one side were France, Russia and Britain – each pledged to defend any attack on their allies. Ranged against them was the might of Germany and the Austro-Hungarian Empire.

KAISER WILHELM II – ambitious to make Germany a great power

KING GEORGE V – British Empire largest in the world

RAYMOND POINCARE – French fear growing threat of Germany

EMPEROR FRANZ JOSEPH – hanging on to Austro-Hungarian empire

TSAR NICHOLAS II OF RUSSIA – largest but poorest country in Europe

As it turned out, the First World War was sparked by events in a little-known town called Sarajevo. On a sunny day in June 1914 Archduke Franz Ferdinand – heir to his daddy's Austro-Hungarian Empire – was visiting a Bosnian town called Sarajevo. It was Ferdy's wedding anniversary and he was looking forward to greeting the cheering crowds of his loyal subjects. It rather spoiled his day when a bomb went off near his carriage. To make matters worse – much worse – his driver took a wrong turning down a narrow street. There, 19-year-old Gavrilo Princip, a member of the Serb terrorists called the Black Hand Gang (yes, really), was waiting. Gavrilo fired two shots from close range and hit the Archduke in the neck. No two shots in history have had such terrible consequences. The trigger-happy Gavrilo showed no remorse.

I am not a criminal, for I destroyed a bad man. I thought I was right.

What happened next was a chain reaction. Austria declared war on Serbia, who asked for Russian help. In retaliation Germany declared war on Russia and France. To attack France, Germany invaded Belgium. Britain was left with little choice but to join in.

KING GEORGE V WRITING DIARY

4ᵗʰ August 1914 – Warm, showers and windy. At work all day. I held a Council at 10.45 to declare war with Germany.

Britain didn't want a war but the government had guaranteed they would help Belgium. More to the point if they stood by, Germany would soon be the dominant power in Europe (instead of Britain).

As for Winston, he was in his element. There were only two members of the Government who had any experience of war. One was the elderly Army Minister with the ferocious moustache, Lord Kitchener. The other was the energetic and excitable Winston Churchill.

Kitchener wasn't much of a man for speeches but Winston was more than happy to speak for them both. He had just turned 40 years old and the stage was set for him to play a starring role.

The twerp of Antwerp

The war didn't start smoothly for Winston. The Allies – Britain, France and Russia – were desperate to save the Belgian coastline from the German advance. The city of Antwerp was under siege and being pounded by German howitzers (a gun that fired shells high into the air). Typically Winston felt that someone ought to go there to see what could be done. Three guesses who volunteered…

WINSTON'S LOST DIARY
4 October 1914

Arrived in Antwerp yesterday. My mission is to assess the situation. I've assessed it and things are desperate. Gallant little Belgium must not be left to its fate. The Belgian army is small, our boys are still arriving and there's no sign of the French yet. Morale is low and no one seems to know what to do.

Someone needs to take command. I've thought it over and I'm the man. Have written to the PM offering to resign my Admiralty post so I can take over here.

Think of it – a general in command of a

great army! Well a small one anyway. To hold out against all the odds and win a great victory. What could be more thrilling?

'Churchill of Antwerp' that's what they'll call me one day.

7 October

Humbug! The Prime Minister has said no. French have still not arrived. Leave for home the day after tomorrow. Without me the city will never hold out.

The day after Winston left, the city of Antwerp surrendered. Prime Minister Asquith had been startled by Winston's wild offer. But he couldn't help admiring his nerve.

He is a wonderful creature, with a curious dash of schoolboy simplicity ... and what someone said of genius – a zigzag streak of lightning in his brain.

Back home other people weren't so kind. They thought that Winston was showing off again. He was wild, a meddler, mad as the moon. Even Clementine had to admit that on this occasion 'Winston's sense of proportion had deserted him'. Winston's critics said he had no business offering to resign from his Admiralty post on a whim. How could he be a government minister one moment and the commander of an army the next? To Winston nothing could be simpler. He still had soldiering in his blood. When someone had to take charge he always felt that he was the best man for the job.

Down the plug in the Dardanelles

If the Antwerp episode made Winston look a fool, then much worse was to come. By 1915 the war was at a stalemate with both sides dug in on the Western Front. The trenches stretched all the way from the English Channel to Switzerland. For the next four years both sides would be locked in a bitter, costly struggle over a few acres of mud.

Winston, who loved military strategy, suggested a different approach. They would attack the enemy in the east. It was simple. Knock Turkey out of the war and supply arms to the Russians through the Dardanelles and the Black Sea, bringing pressure on the German Army from the east. Winston was convinced it would work and managed to persuade all the other members of the War Cabinet. Big mistake.

In 1915 the attack began with a naval bombardment of Gallipoli on the west coast of Turkey. Winston believed it would win the day. Actually it was a total failure. To make matters worse, a great land assault was launched – and failed. The story was one disaster after another. In the history of war, Gallipoli is right up there with almighty clangers like the Charge of the Light Brigade.

'Mad' Admiral Fisher, who Winston had unwisely brought back, resigned in the middle of the campaign, leaving Winston to take the blame. It wasn't really fair, but the public wanted a scapegoat. When the red-faced government invited the Conservatives to join them, Winston's old party saw their chance to put the boot in. They hadn't forgotten how the young upstart had once walked out on them, now it was their chance to get even.

Thanks to the Conservatives, Winston lost his job and his hat at the Admiralty. He was shunted into a new post as Chancellor of the Duchy of Lancaster – a job that involved long hours of thumb twiddling. At the age of 40 Winston's brilliant career looked washed up.

Mud, glorious mud

There was only one thing for it. Politics had relegated him to the sidelines, so he would return to the Army. Winston was rather like a cork in the sea, he was bound to bob up again eventually.

In November 1915 Winston, though still an MP, travelled to the Western Front to experience life in the trenches for himself. He didn't know how long he would stay but it was a bold decision when men in France were dying in their thousands. Death didn't worry Winston, he couldn't spend the rest of the war as a spectator, he had to do something active.

The Western Front certainly offered action. Winston had arrived without a command but through the influence of General Haig, Commander in Chief, he was eventually made a lieutenant colonel with the Royal Scots Fusiliers. At first the soldiers he commanded gave him a frosty reception. What was a balding, middle-aged politician doing in the trenches? Trying to play the hero and save his career? They soon changed their tune. Winston was prepared to share all the misery of trench life and won them over with his cheerfulness and energy. His diary would have had plenty to record.

WINSTON'S LOST WAR DIARY
Nov 21 1915

My first two days in the trenches. Filth and rubbish everywhere! Water and muck on all sides! Graves are built into our defences, and feet and dead men's clothes stick out of the mud. My trench is only two feet six inches high so we have to crawl in like dogs.

At night gigantic bats creep out and glide in the moonlight to the angry noise of

machine guns and the whine of bullets
passing overhead.

Am sure I'll enjoy my six months out
here. Have never felt so happy in my
life!

Jan 4 1916

This afternoon I gathered my men
together and told them, 'Gentlemen we
are going to make war - on the lice! The
nasty little bugs get everywhere. We
used some brewery vats to boil the
water. I think all the officers were
amazed and impressed that it worked.
Naturally I tried not to look too pleased
with myself.

Jan 16 1916

No action at the moment. This evening I
organized a sports day and concert for
the men. Many of them are young and
have never been to war. I think the poor
fellows need nursing more than a drill

sergeant barking at them. We had mule races, pillow fights, and obstacle races, rounded off with a banquet and a topping concert. You never heard such singing - though no one had the faintest idea of the tune.

A LIFE IN HATS

Number 3: LIEUTENANT COLONEL

While he was at the front, Winston was made the present of a French steel helmet which he took to wearing with boyish glee. 'I look most martial in it – like a Cromwellian,' he said. 'I intend to wear it under fire – but chiefly for appearance.'

A charmed life

Winston spent six months at the front before he decided he was needed back in Parliament. He survived his time in the trenches – but only just. As ever he seemed to believe he would survive because his life's work wasn't finished yet. Destiny still called. However if he was hit by a bullet or a shell – well then his time was up, there was no sense in worrying about it. (Back home, Clemmie worried enough for both of them.)

On several occasions the ex-Minister seemed to lead a charmed life. Once he was called out to a meeting with a General at a crossroads. When Winston finally got there, he received a message saying the General was sorry but he couldn't make it that day. Winston cursed the General all the way back to his trench, only to find that it had been blown up in his absence – the shell exploding a few feet from where he would have been sitting.

Near the end of his posting, Winston was sitting in a farm with his officers drinking coffee and port. Suddenly there was a tremendous crash with dust and splinters flying everywhere. Winston had been playing with his lamp before the blast. He noticed that a piece of shrapnel (bomb case) had almost split the metal lamp in two – missing his hand by only two inches.

Before he left, Winston made a speech to his officers about how to conduct themselves in a war. The list tells you more about Winston than the war itself.

WINSTON'S CODE OF CONDUCT FOR OFFICERS

1 Don't be careless about yourselves. On the other hand don't be too careful.

2 Keep a special pair of boots to sleep in and only get them muddy in an emergency.

3 Drink alcohol in moderation – don't have a great parade of bottles in your dugouts.

4 Live well but do not flaunt it.

5 Teach your men to laugh. War is a game played with a smile. ⟶

6 If you can't smile, grin. If you can't grin, keep out of the way until you can.

Tanks a million

While Winston was at the Western Front his restless mind wasn't idle. He was always dreaming of new inventions to improve the war effort. In the autumn of 1914, near the beginning of the war, a brilliant lieutenant colonel called E D Swinton had come up with the idea of an armoured vehicle, a sort of battleship on land. No one paid much attention to such a crackpot idea, except Winston. While he was First Lord of the Admiralty he took up the suggestion, dreaming of a vehicle that could plough over heavy mud and barbed wire with the machine-gun fire bouncing off it like raindrops.

When he served at the Western Front and saw that troops trying to take German machine-gun posts were sitting ducks, Winston remembered Swinton's idea. Largely thanks to Churchill's influence the first experimental machines started to arrive in France in 1916. The tank was born.

Tanks didn't play a vital part in the First World War, partly because the stuffed shirts leading the war lacked the imagination to see their possibilities. Admittedly the early Mark One tanks were slow cumbersome machines that needed to stop before they could turn in a different direction. One early model had many defects and teething troubles, 'When these became apparent it was rechristened "The Churchill",' reported Winston cheerfully.

THE MARK ONE TANK

CARRIES TWO HOTCHKISS GUNS AND FOUR MACHINE GUNS

106 HORSEPOWER ENGINE

TOP SPEED - A LIGHTNING 4 MILES AN HOUR

TAIL WHEEL MEANT TO AID BALANCE - UTTERLY USELESS

CATERPILLAR TRACKS

INSIDE: THREE DRIVERS AND FOUR GUNNERS - HOT, NOISY AND SUFFOCATING

MEN WERE OFTEN VIOLENTLY SICK AFTER A SHORT JOURNEY!

Winston's soldiering days were over. In May 1916 he left the Western Front and was sadly missed by all those officers who had greeted his arrival with loud boos.

By the summer of 1916 he returned to Parliament, though still as an outsider. The government was making a hopeless mess of the war and Winston felt the time had come to speak out. Unlike most MPs he could speak of the war from first-hand experience. In less than a year he was back in the War Cabinet, his return greeted by howls of protest from the Conservatives.

For the remainder of the war, Winston was put in charge of munitions (weapons to you and me) and set about the task with his usual dynamic energy. By 1918 the German Army was defeated and the First World War was drawing to a close. Winston was back at the top and throughout the 1920s his name would rarely be out of the headlines. He still believed that great things lay ahead.

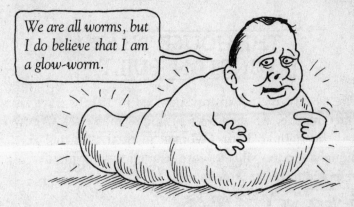

We are all worms, but I do believe that I am a glow-worm.

THE HOUSE THAT WINSTON BUILT

The world which Winston surveyed in 1918 was a very different one. All men over 21 and women over 30 now had the right to vote. (Women in their twenties were thought far too silly to vote, though young men were supposed to be far more mature.)

I VOTE WE ALL WEAR OUR PANTS ON OUR HEADS!

Giving ordinary people the right to vote may sound an obvious step, but in 1918 it was a revolution. The world had been turned upside down. Now men and women from the shipyards and cotton mills had a say in who would govern the country. The world was no longer entirely ruled by toffs in top hats – like Winston Churchill.

WINSTON'S WORLD: WORKERS AND WOMEN

Remember the suffragettes campaigning for the vote in the 1900s? In the end their protests did them little good. What won women the vote was the part they'd played in the war. With the men away at the front, someone had to take on all the jobs that were left vacant. Women stepped in to the breach to become nurses and factory workers for the first time and after the war no one could deny them the right to vote. (Of course they had to give back their jobs to the returning soldiers.)

Women weren't the only ones who were looking forward to making their voices heard. After 1918 a vast number of working men got the vote. The Labour Party which had started with just one MP, threatened now to become a real power in politics. Churchill sniffed revolution in the air and didn't like the smell.

Fit for heroes

In 1918 the 'khaki' election was held – so called because khaki was the colour worn by thousands of returning soldiers. Despite the growing influence of the Labour Party, Lloyd George's coalition of Tories and Liberals held on to power and promised to make a 'land fit for heroes'.

Winston was in his element as Minister for War and Air. You would have though this was a dead-end job since the war was over, but Churchill was never busier.

For one thing he took up flying lessons again. Yes, he was supposed to have given up flying but aeroplanes, said Winston, were so much safer than they used to be.

Just to prove it he nearly killed himself taking off from Croydon Airport. His family begged him to put aside his pilot's goggles for good.

No cheers

The 1920s would be a rollercoaster ride for Winston. The 'land fit for heroes' the government had promised was really hardly fit for a dog.

It was time for working men and women to make their voices heard.

In October 1922, the Prime Minister Lloyd George resigned and an election was held. It was a disaster for Churchill which left him shaken in more ways than one.

As voting day drew near, Winston went down with a nasty case of appendicitis. In those days appendicitis was a serious illness – painkillers weren't very effective and having your appendix out was a risky operation.

Winston survived but had to campaign for his seat in Dundee having just crawled from his hospital bed. Clementine bravely went up to Scotland to see what her charm and intelligence could do. Not much, as it turned out. The women of Dundee, whose husbands and sons were out of work, gave a rowdy reception to the well-spoken English lady. As one witness reported: 'Clemmie appeared with a string of pearls. The women spat on her.'

Winston dragged himself north of the border for the last four days of the election campaign, but he might as well have stayed at home.

WINSTON'S LOST DIARY
12 November 1922

Big speech at the Drill Hall in Dundee yesterday. I was carried through the yelling crowd to the platform. Talk about entering the lion's den! Every face seemed to be shouting at me. If I hadn't been so weak I think they probably would have attacked me.

Felt dreadfully sick and ill. Even standing up leaves me exhausted. I was booed, hissed, heckled and interrupted. And that was just the opening line of my speech.

HISS

BOO   BOO

On polling day Churchill was defeated by vast numbers of poor women and mill workers who had never voted before. They queued round the block to cast their votes. His majority of 15,000 was overturned and he was beaten by 10,000 votes.

Winston was left...

Without an office, without a seat, without a party and without an appendix.

For the first time in 17 years Winston was out of Parliament. Maybe it was a blessing in disguise – 'what I want now is a rest,' he admitted.

He'd had little time for Clemmie and his children during the war and now he was given a year or two to recharge his batteries. There were other things in life besides politics and Winston was not someone who lacked outside interests. At various stages of his life he found time for polo, painting, bricklaying, swimming, hunting, gambling, flying lessons and keeping a farmyard of animals (more about them later). In his spare time Winston made a very good living from writing books. The first volume of his next book appeared in April 1923 – a history of the First World War which filled a modest 2,000 pages. Of course, when Winston wrote about history, it was strictly his own version.

Winston has written a book about himself and called it The World Crisis.

Arthur Balfour (Conservative Minister)

Meet the Churchills

By 1923 Winston and Clemmie had a growing family of four. It would have been five but their third daughter Marigold had sadly died two years earlier.

In some ways Winston was a good father. Being a big kid himself, he understood children. Sometimes he would play 'gorillas' with them in the garden, dropping from a tree and beating his chest before they ran off shrieking with delight as he chased them.

Yet, as they grew up, having Winston Churchill for a father wasn't easy. Winston himself had suffered from never being able to please his father and didn't want to make the same mistakes with his own children. But somehow they ran into trouble anyway. Perhaps it was because he had such high expectations for them. When Diana, the eldest, was born Winston wrote to Clemmie that, 'She ought to have some rare qualities of both mind and body.' Diana would prove as headstrong as her father by marrying a man her parents didn't approve of.

Winston referred to his second daughter, red-headed Sarah, as 'the mule' because he said she was very obstinate. Sarah insisted on a career on the stage, upsetting her parents doubly when she married a radio comedian. Only Mary, the baby of the family, was an easy child who loved horses and did well at school.

Despite this, Winston pinned most of his hopes on young Randolph. After all, in the 1920s it was still men who really counted in society. Randolph was dashingly handsome and took it for granted that he was destined for great things like his famous father. To prove it he dropped out of Oxford University at the age of 19 and launched himself on a lecture tour of America. Randolph had Winston's brash self-confidence, but unfortunately he lacked both his talent and his charm. He soon developed a reputation for rudeness and arrogance.

It frustrated Winston that nearly all his children stubbornly steered their own course in life, ignoring all advice. In this they were just like their father.

Home sweet hovel
In the autumn of 1922 Winston made a momentous decision that would affect the rest of his life. He bought a house.

WINSTON'S LOST DIARY

October 20 1922

I am in love! Drove out to Chartwell in the rolling Kent countryside and on first sight I knew I couldn't resist her. The house looks out over a valley and miles and miles of perfect English countryside.

Of course it's in a bit of a mess. The roof leaks, the wiring is medieval and there may be a touch of dry rot. It faces the wrong way too - north instead of south. But these are mere details. What a cosy home it will be when it's finished (and a real bargain too at less than £5,000.)

Haven't told Clemmie yet. I'm sure she will be delighted. ———>

October 22

Clemmie furious. Called the house an 'ugly wreck'.

Winston looked at Chartwell like a general surveying a battlefield and planning his victory. Clemmie looked at it as someone who would have to live there and bring up a young family. She knew it would be expensive to rebuild and to run. In fact there was so much work to do that it took over a year before the family could actually move in.

Chartwell would become Winston's refuge and his HQ. It was where he held court. From the 1920s onwards, his friends, admirers and political allies made the hour-long trip from London to Chartwell to see the great man. Clemmie was driven mad by Winston often announcing at the last moment…

Over the next 30 years Chartwell almost bled Winston dry – he spent £18,000 on rebuilding the house and gardens – in those days a small fortune. His triumph was to transform it from a crumbling heap into an English manor house.

You can still go and visit Churchill's family home at Chartwell today. It's easy to imagine him striding through the grounds in his smock and straw hat, off to paint that spectacular view.

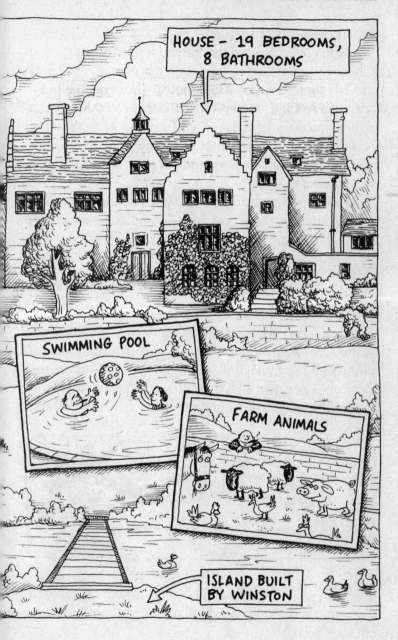

Four-legged friends

Winston once admitted that he had few friends, although Chartwell was always buzzing with people. At heart maybe he preferred animals since he surrounded himself with every kind of four-legged beast. Winston was a typical country gentleman and saw no contradiction between keeping pigs as pets and hunting them in India. 'You carve the goose, Clemmie,' he once instructed. 'He was a friend of mine.'

There are many stories about Winston and animals. A good source of them was his long-suffering secretary, Grace Hamblin, who had to look after Winston's mad menagerie as well as keep up with his letters.

Dogs

Winston's pet dogs were two poodles called Rufus One and Rufus Two. They were both pampered and indulged. Rufus ate with the family in the dining room at Chartwell. A tablecloth was laid out for him on the Persian carpet next to Churchill's chair and nobody was allowed to start eating until the butler had served Rufus his food.

Pigs

Winston was especially fond of pigs, whom he thought charming and intelligent. Unlike some people he knew.

Dogs look up to us, cats look down on us, pigs treat us as equals.

Winston was delighted when Grace Hamblin's father fixed a wire to the end of a pole and gave it to him as a back scratcher for his pig.

Budgies

Another pet was a green budgerigar called Toby who was given the freedom of the house at Chartwell. Sometimes the bird would fly into the dining room where he had to be prevented from pecking the salt which was bad for budgies. Instead it would fly down and often perch on a visitor's head. Winston was grief-stricken when Toby flew off during a stay in the south of France and didn't return.

Cats

Winston always had a cat or two including a favourite marmalade one called Ginger. One of Churchill's cats was a rather snooty character and once went off in a huff.

GOOD MORNING, CAT!

I SAID 'GOOD MORNING, CAT!'

YAWN!

YEEEOW!

WHACK

93

Fish

Winston created a series of ponds and lakes in his garden where he liked to keep fish and black swans. Once, on Winston's birthday, a little boy of about ten years old arrived at the door of his London house with an unusual present – a tin of tropical fish called black mollies. They were the beginning of Winston's fascination with tropical fish. By the time he was Prime Minister he had a collection which filled five tanks. Winston also kept golden orfe, which are rather like large goldfish, in his ponds. Their diet included live maggots brought specially by train from a town in Yorkshire. Every now and then the phone would ring from the station at Westerham and the porter would declare:

Whose side am I on?

Back in the beastly world of politics, Winston was about to swap sides – again.

Remember that in 1904 he deserted the Conservative Party and crossed over to the Liberals? In the eyes of Tories that was about as low as you could stoop, without actually lying in the gutter. Now times had changed and Winston was disenchanted with the Liberal Party. Most MPs joined a party and stuck with it through thick and thin, but Winston wasn't most MPs. He was far more interested in what he believed in than which party he belonged to.

When he was a Liberal Winston declared:

The Conservative Party is not a party but a conspiracy.

Later he acidly remarked:

The Tory fault [is] a yearning for mediocrity.

But in 1923 he decided:

I am what I have always been, a Tory Democrat.

Did this mean that Winston had rediscovered a yearning to be mediocre and middle of the road? Far from it. In the 1924 election Churchill stood independently as an Anti-Socialist candidate in Epping. The local Conservatives adopted him as their candidate and he was elected. The way was now clear for him to rejoin his old Conservative Party again. Many of his old enemies were gone and the new Prime Minister, Stanley Baldwin, realized it was better to have Winston on your side than against you. He was back in his natural home and landed the plum job of Chancellor of the Exchequer. Forty years earlier his father had – briefly – held the same high position.

A striking problem

The mid 1920s were not a peaceful time for the new government. In May 1926 they were faced with the biggest strike in British history. It all started with the coal miners. Already poorly paid, their wages were cut further because of falling coal prices. The miners refused to accept the cuts and in response the owners closed the mines. Two days later the Trade Union Congress called a general strike in support of the miners. With printers, rail workers, bus drivers and dockers downing tools, the country was facing a crisis.

Winston had some sympathy with the miners but was against the strike. He saw it as a threat to the power of Parliament. The country was deeply divided – some people supported the strike, while others volunteered to keep the trams, trains and fire brigade running.

Churchill's own contribution was to organize the printing of a daily paper – the *National Gazette* – which naturally trumpeted the government's side of the argument. He did it in his usual interfering style: 'He butts in at the busiest hours and insists on changing commas and full stops until the staff is furious,' complained H A Gwynne the editor. After only nine days of the General Strike the paper had good news – good news for the government anyway:

THE NATIONAL GAZETTE

May 12 1926

IT'S OVER!
STRIKE CRUMBLES

This morning the General Strike was called off by the Trade Union Congress. During the past nine days thousands of volunteers have bravely kept the trams and trains running, and maintained law and order as police and firemen. The *Gazette* salutes their gallant contribution. In Plymouth, strikers and police were on such good terms that they played football in the streets. In other places we regret to report that trams were overturned and damaged by hooligans.

It's time now to get back to work and let the country return to peace.

Smiling workers return to work.

Many accused Winston Churchill of being an enemy of the working man because he fought against the General Strike. But, in fact, it would have been difficult to find anyone in the government who supported the strike. When it was over Churchill did everything he could to improve the pay of the miners, but the real enemy were the coal owners who stubbornly refused to listen. In the end the miners were forced to accept the cuts.

Throughout the second half of the 1920s Churchill was at the peak of his career. As Chancellor of the Exchequer he was responsible for Britain's national piggy bank and only one rung below the Prime Minister on the political ladder. But it wasn't to last.

In 1929 the Conservatives narrowly lost the election to Ramsay Macdonald's Labour Party. He was out of power and would stay in the shadows for ten long years. The wilderness years had begun.

TIMELINE 2 — THE GLORY YEARS

**1931-39 – OUT IN THE COLD –
THE WILDERNESS YEARS.**

**1936 – BACKS THE WRONG
SIDE IN ABDICATION CRISIS.**

A FIVER ON THE KING!

£5·00

**1939 – WAR DECLARED
ON GERMANY.**

WAR

WAR!

**1939 – WINSTON IS BACK!
THE ADMIRALTY AGAIN.**

**1940 – NORWEGIAN CAMPAIGN
DISASTER.**

NORWAY
DISASTER!

**1940 – PRIME MINISTER
AT 65.**

10

1940 - BATTLE OF BRITAIN.
1940 - BRITS SURVIVE THE BLITZ.
1941 - JAPAN BOMBS PEARL HARBOR - ENTER AMERICA.
1941-42 - BATTLE OF THE ATLANTIC. U-BOAT MENACE.
THEY'RE BRINGING ON A SUB!
1942 - BATTLE OF EL-ALAMEIN. DESERT RATS BITE BACK.
KABOOM!
1944 - D-DAY. ALLIES STORM NORMANDY BEACHES.

WINSTON IN THE WILDERNESS

By 1930 Winston had reached the age of 56, late middle age. There was certainly more of him around the middle than there used to be.

PORKY WINSTON AT 50

PINK SKIN

BALD HEAD

MISCHIEVOUS GRIN

CHUBBY FACE

EVER-PRESENT CIGAR

BIT OF A PORKER - 15 STONE

You'll remember Churchill once said that all babies looked like him. It was true – but now he was a big wrinkly baby. Heading for his sixties, most people thought he couldn't be far from retirement. The old boy had had an impressive career – war hero, best-selling writer, First Lord of the Admiralty and Chancellor of the Exchequer. It wasn't a bad innings, but now his best years were behind him. People said this behind his back. They couldn't have been more wrong – at the age of 56, Winston was still warming up.

To the new generation of MPs it must have seemed that Winston had passed his sell-by date. While he was a familiar face in Parliament, no one wanted him in government. Winston often had a bee in his bonnet about something or other and this time it was India. In Winston's childhood, India was the crown jewel of the British Empire. As a young man he'd served there in the Army, but now the country was marching towards independence. Almost everyone accepted the fact except Churchill, who could bore for England on the subject of India remaining in the Empire. This backward-looking stance made him look like an old fossil, totally out of step with the times. Churchill was still one of the great speech-makers, but during the 1930s no one was really listening.

The high life

Out of favour in politics, Winston turned to his home-life, his many hobbies and his book writing. The books would save him from poverty – or at least from having to cut down on cigars and champagne. From his books he earned vast sums – in 1929, £40,000 from journalism alone (£650,000 today). It should have made him rich but it didn't. He had a whopping overdraft with the bank and despite occasional half-hearted attempts to cut back on heating or phone bills, there never seemed to be enough money (a complaint he first made as a schoolboy). Winston was made for the high life and for much of his middle age he was teetering on the edge of bankruptcy.

How did he manage to spend so much? Chartwell was largely to blame. At his country house he couldn't manage without an army of servants. Eight or nine for indoors plus a nanny, two secretaries, a chauffeur, three gardeners, a groom for the horses and a bailiff to run the estate. Winston lived in the grand manner of a country gentleman – as the grandson of a duke, he couldn't possibly be expected to do anything for himself. That was the whole point of having servants! Once he arrived on holiday in the Riviera and told his astonished hostess.

Servants were there to find out the times of trains, to pack his bag and drive him wherever he wanted. Servants ran the bath for Winston, dried him, dressed him, brought him cigars and drinks. They even pulled on his socks for him! Churchill was like an emperor, clapping his hands when he entered the house for his servants to come running. He was only happy when he was being pampered and cosseted like a child. If he felt he was being neglected there was trouble brewing. Servants described his expression as glaring, glowering or scowling. At these times Winston was less like an angry bulldog and more like a pampered pig.

Sometimes if there was a group of servants, Churchill would move along the line, scowling at them one by one as if they were a scruffy regiment on parade. Once, when a male nurse was slow to obey instructions, he had to duck quickly to avoid a pair of hairbrushes flying past his head.

Churchill's three secretaries probably suffered the most. Winston would dictate to them at all times of the day and during whatever he was doing. Sometimes they had to climb a ladder and take notes while Winston was at the top laying bricks.

Churchill stayed at the best hotels, ate at the finest restaurants, smoked the finest Havana cigars and drank only the best champagne, port and brandy. Once the manager of the Plaza Hotel in New York where Winston was due to stay, telephoned to ask about the great man's tastes. Winston himself answered the call and replied:

'He knows nothing of the life of ordinary people,' Clementine once remarked quite truthfully. Winston never went on a bus or shopped by himself. The only time he tried to travel on the London Underground was during the General Strike and then he went round and round in circles, getting hopelessly confused. He might have been there for ever if someone hadn't taken pity on him.

Nine till twelve

When at Chartwell, Winston had a set routine which rarely varied. He crammed more into a day than most people managed in a week. His amazing energy he put down to his habit of taking an afternoon siesta. Bed and food feature a lot in Winston's daily timetable, but he would also sometimes work until three in the morning.

A DAY IN THE LIFE

<u>8am:</u> Wake up. A modest breakfast in bed. Bacon and eggs, a leg of chicken, toast, marmalade and coffee.

<u>9-11 am:</u> Read mail and all the papers in bed. Dictate letters to a secretary - they're used to seeing me in my pyjamas.

<u>11 am:</u> Time to get up. First bath of the day and perhaps a walk round the garden. A weak whisky and soda then back to work.

<u>1 pm:</u> Lunch time! I make it a rule always to be late for lunch. Guests like to see you make a big entrance. Lunch is a proper three-course meal. Nothing fancy - perhaps oysters, fillet of sole wrapped in smoked salmon and roast venison

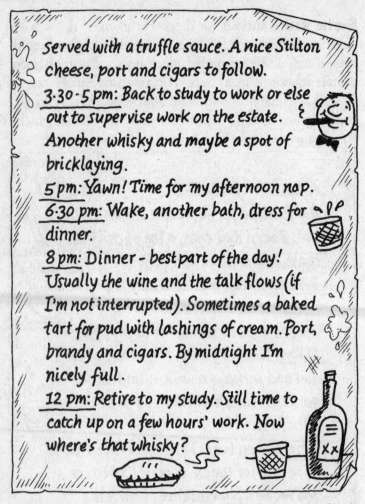

served with a truffle sauce. A nice Stilton cheese, port and cigars to follow.

3.30 - 5 pm: Back to study to work or else out to supervise work on the estate. Another whisky and maybe a spot of bricklaying.

5 pm: Yawn! Time for my afternoon nap.

6.30 pm: Wake, another bath, dress for dinner.

8 pm: Dinner - best part of the day! Usually the wine and the talk flows (if I'm not interrupted). Sometimes a baked tart for pud with lashings of cream. Port, brandy and cigars. By midnight I'm nicely full.

12 pm: Retire to my study. Still time to catch up on a few hours' work. Now where's that whisky?

You might think that with all that rich food, champagne, whisky and cigars, Winston's lifestyle was not exactly healthy. And you'd be right. Certainly Winston had a bit of a weight problem. For a shortish man he looked like a pocket battleship. Occasionally he tried dieting – swapping big meals for milk and biscuits –

but he wasn't cut out for diets. He liked to drink with every meal but he didn't like getting drunk. On the one occasion the MP Bessie Braddock accused him of being drunk, she was treated to his famous put down.

Winston smoked nine or ten of his cigars a day and had a collection which grew to an astonishing 3,000 – mostly gifts from friends and admirers. In fact he probably didn't smoke as much as people imagined because he had a habit of playing with cigars rather than smoking them. Winston would chew on them, light and relight them until finally he threw them away only half-smoked.

Maybe the cigar was partly there as a prop – a trademark that made him instantly recognizable. Just as Hitler had his funny little moustache, Winston had his collection of hats and his cigars.

Dog days

Winston's most serious health problem was nothing to do with smoking or drinking, it was the depression that sometimes descended on him like a dark cloud. Winston called it his 'black dog'. Possibly depression ran in the family – five Dukes of Marlborough suffered from melancholy and Winston's own father Randolph had moods that went up and down like a yo-yo. Winston's black dog followed at his heels whenever things were going badly or when he didn't have enough to occupy him. He didn't like to think too much about his mistakes because he found he couldn't live with them. When he was younger a period of depression had lasted for two or three years and only talking to Clemmie helped him through. It was no exaggeration to say that Churchill sometimes thought about ending it all.

I don't like standing near the edge of a platform when an express train is passing… A second's action would end everything.

HOBBIES WITH WINSTON: BRICKS AND PAINT

Winston's mind needed occupation and he turned to his hobbies – practical and artistic.

Bricklaying was a trade he took to with enthusiasm. Once he had mastered the technique, he claimed he could lay 60 bricks an hour. At Chartwell he built a house for his butler – and then went on to build two cottages and a playhouse for his daughter Mary, all with his own hands. A good day for Winston meant 2,000 words written and 200 bricks laid.

Painting was even more of a passion. His first brush with art came in 1915 when he had just left the Admiralty. Staying for a weekend at Hoe Farm with his sister-in-law, Goonie, he watched her painting one day. Winston was fascinated and eagerly accepted her invitation to have a go. At first he approached the canvas timidly, unsure how to build up a picture. What saved him was advice from Hazel Lavery, the wife of a famous painter, who told him that boldness and audacity were essential for an artist. Boldness? That was Winston's middle name! He began to attack the canvas with wild strokes and slashes. Painting was the only thing that Winston did in total silence, completely absorbed in the task before him. When he set out to paint at Chartwell, he was like a general riding out to battle.

WINSTON PAINTS A PICTURE

111

Churchill liked to paint landscapes, but he wasn't above making changes for dramatic effect. Once his friend Violet Bonham-Carter watched him paint a rather dull, flat landscape. In Winston's picture, however, the view was improved by a range of impressive mountains. 'Well I couldn't leave it as dull as all that,' he explained.

Was he any good? Quite likely Winston didn't care one way or the other, but he did once submit his work to the famous Louvre Gallery in Paris and was good enough to be accepted (under a false name so that no one could claim he was cheating).

Friends like these...

Although he knew a lot of people, Winston claimed he had few real friends. Perhaps it was due to his habit of saying rude things about almost everyone. It didn't seem to matter whether they were Tory, Liberal or Labour – most politicians felt the lash of Winston's tongue at some point or other.

WINSTON ON POLITICIANS

ARTHUR BALFOUR-
Conservative Prime
Minister 1902-06

If you wanted
nothing done, Arthur
Balfour was the man
for the task.

STANLEY BALDWIN-
Conservative Prime
Minister 1923-24,
1924-29, 1935-37

He has his ear so close
to the ground that he
has locusts in it.

CLEMENT ATLEE-
Labour PM 1945-51

A modest man who
has a great deal
to be modest about.

CHARLES De GAULLE-
President of France 1958-69

He looks like a female
llama who has just
been surprised in
her bath.

If Winston was careless in making enemies, he wasn't much better at choosing his friends. He was drawn to colourful, larger-than-life characters with strong opinions. People like himself in fact. Clemmie nicknamed three of his best pals 'The Terrible B's' – Beaverbrook, Bracken and Birkenhead. The odd man out in Churchill's cronies was Frederick Lindemann – and not just because his name didn't begin with a B. Professor Lindemann was a quietly spoken scientist, a strict vegetarian who would remove the yolks from eggs before eating them.

CHURCHILL AT DINNER WITH HIS PALS
(AND TOY CAT)

LORD BEAVERBROOK
(MAX AITKEN)
CANADIAN SCOT, TORY MP WHO LATER BECAME A NEWSPAPER MOGUL. CHURCHILL DISAGREED WITH HIM ON ALMOST EVERYTHING, BUT NEVERTHELESS LIKED HIS 'FOUL-WEATHER FRIEND'.

LORD BIRKENHEAD
(FE SMITH)
BECAME PALS WITH CHURCHILL WHEN FIRST AN MP IN 1906. FIERCE INTELLECTUAL WHOSE SHARP TONGUE MADE EVEN WINSTON LOOK LIKE A PUSSY CAT. DIED EARLY, AGED 58, DESPITE TRYING TO GIVE UP THE DEMON DRINK.

With Lord Birkenhead, Winston founded 'The Other Club' – a dinner club which met every other Thursday at the Savoy in London. Churchill always sat in pride of place at the middle of the table with his back to the Thames. To join The Other Club you had to be invited and it helped to be one of Winston's pals or at least one of his toadies. If only 13 members arrived to dinner it was a tradition that a fourteenth was brought in to ward off bad luck. The 14th member was a large black toy cat.

BRENDAN BRACKEN
JOURNALIST, BANKER AND TORY MP AT THE TENDER AGE OF 28. VISITED CHURCHILL SO OFTEN AT WEEKENDS THAT SUNDAYS WERE KNOWN AS 'BRACKEN DAYS'. RUMOUR SPREAD THAT BRACKEN WAS SECRETLY CHURCHILL'S SON FROM AN AFFAIR. CLEMMIE WAS NOT AMUSED.

FREDERICK LINDEMANN
BRILLIANT SCIENTIST KNOWN AS 'THE PROF'. TEETOTAL, NON-SMOKER WHO BECAME CHURCHILL'S PERSONAL THINK TANK FROM THE 1930S ON. 'SCIENTISTS SHOULD BE ON TAP NOT ON TOP,' SAID WINSTON.

Suffering Clemmie

Clemmie never really liked any of Winston's pals (perhaps with the exception of Lindemann). She thought they only added to Winston's reputation for being a colourful crackpot, someone who couldn't really be trusted in government.

On Clementine fell the burden of managing Chartwell and entertaining Winston's procession of guests – all on a shoestring budget. She had never asked to live in a grand house in the first place and Winston's reckless spending often drove her potty. Once, when they argued over how they could cut back, Clementine threw a plate of spinach at Winston which missed and hit the wall.

Most of the time she found it was useless to argue with him since he would always shout her down. If she had something to communicate she found it best to write him a note.

At times Clemmie was worn out by the demands her husband made on her and would have to spend time away to recover. Without her Winston was a ship adrift and wrote her letters begging her to return as soon as possible.

There is no doubt that 'Pig' and 'Kat' loved each other but it was a marriage conducted entirely on Winston's terms. Sometimes she would recite the lines she claimed would be written on her grave:

CLEMENTINE CHURCHILL

Here lies a woman who was always tired, For she lived in a world where too much was required

A right royal blunder

Winston could boast royalty among his friends, in particular the heir to the throne, Edward, Prince of Wales. Like many of Winston's friendships it only brought him trouble. Churchill had hit it off with the Prince as early as 1913 and said of him, 'He is so nice and we have made rather friends… He requires to fall in love with a pretty cat.'

Edward found his cat in 1935 when he met and fell in love with the American, Mrs Wallis Warfield Simpson. However she wasn't the kind of bride a future king was supposed to marry – not only was she American, she was about to leave her second husband. British kings were not allowed to marry divorced women. In 1935 the relationship would have caused a scandal, except that everyone – including the newspapers – kept it a secret. In Europe and America 'the Edward and Wallis affair' was gossiped at every dinner table, but incredibly most people in Britain knew nothing about it.

The crisis broke in December 1936 when the government made it plain the King must choose between the throne and marrying Wallis Simpson.

Churchill made a king-size blunder in trying to intervene. He never really believed Edward would marry Wallis Simpson and wildly overestimated the support for the young king. When Winston tried to argue the King's case in the House of Commons on 7 December he was shouted down. Edward handed the throne to his younger brother and stepped into the shadows. Meanwhile Winston had shot himself in the foot, just when he looked like gaining acceptance again. As Harold Nicolson noted in his diary, 'He has undermined in five minutes the patient reconstruction work of five years.'

117

In a special cupboard at Chartwell Winston kept his startling hat collection. He had dozens of hats. From the beginning he always loved dressing up in uniform and kept his headgear from his army and navy days, as well as adding to his collection on his travels around the world. Winston complained: 'Cartoonists … have dwelt on my hats; how many there are, how strange and queer; and how I am always changing them … and so on. It is all rubbish…' Yet the business with the hats was started by Winston himself. Hats were as much a part of his character as his famous cigar. If he'd wanted to he could have staged his own hat fashion show.

But there remained one hat that Winston had never worn. The hat of a Prime Minister. After ten years in the wilderness, most people thought his chance had long gone – especially after he'd backed the wrong side in the royal crisis. But a far-worse storm was brewing across the Channel and it was blowing in Winston's direction. The Second World War was about to begin.

WINSTON V HITLER

It all started with the rise of a little man with a toothbrush moustache. Adolf Hitler couldn't have been more of a contrast to Winston Churchill.

HITLER

CHURCHILL

The differences were pretty obvious – Hitler had a lot more hair than Churchill, while Winston looked heavy enough to squash Hitler if he ever sat on him. Sadly they didn't have the opportunity to test this out. On the only occasion they were due to meet before the war, Hitler didn't turn up.

One thing they had in common was a magnetic presence. Hitler had startling light-blue eyes and people felt he could see right through them. Although he was short-sighted,

Hitler never wore glasses in public. One of his tricks was to stare people out without blinking. He once engaged in a staring duel with Albert Speer over dinner which might have gone on for ever if they hadn't been interrupted.

Churchill was just as dominating – though he used words rather than a fixed stare. In addition he was much less bothered about his appearance than Hitler. The *Führer* hated to be seen naked by anyone and wore white long johns to cover himself under his uniform. Churchill in contrast quite often met people in his dressing gown or even straight out of the bath!

When it came to making speeches, both men were masters of their art. They could hold a crowd spellbound and stir their hearts within them. But their aims were entirely different.

WINSTON'S WORLD: THE NARZEES

Who were the Nazis – or Narzees, as Winston insisted on calling them?

Nazi was a shortened name for the *Nationalsozialistiche Deutsche Arbeiterpartei* – or the National Socialist German Workers Party. The party leader might have been Adolf Schickelgruber if his father hadn't changed the family name to Hitler in 1876. ('Heil, Schickelgruber!' doesn't really roll off the tongue.) Hitler joined the Nazis in 1919 and quickly rose to be its leader by his charisma and genius.

When the Nazis came to power, few Germans really understood the true nature of their ideas – and by the time they realized it was too late. Hitler wanted to create a master race of blue-eyed, fair-haired *Aryans* who would rule the world. In order to make Germany 'racially pure' he planned to weed out Jews, Communists and gypsies and later came up with the 'Final Solution' to exterminate them. Other races would be allowed to serve the master race once they had been conquered.

After 1932 when the Nazis were voted into power Hitler systematically crushed all the other political parties. He became known as the *Führer* (leader) and soon elections were a thing of the past. Adolf Schickelgruber had already come a long way but his mad ambition was about to shake the whole world.

Please, Mr Hitler

From the early 1930s Churchill started to beat the drum of warning against the growing Nazi threat. Germany was building a massive army and an air force to rival Britain's RAF (Royal Air Force).

By 1938 it was clear that Hitler planned a lot more than merely restoring Germany to the Germans. The Nazi Army marched into Austria and then Czechoslovakia. The question was, what were France and Britain going to do about it?

The answer was: nothing. Successive British Prime Ministers in the 1930s – Ramsay Macdonald, Stanley Baldwin and, most famously, Neville Chamberlain – refused to listen to Churchill's dire warnings and followed a policy known as 'appeasement'. In short this meant not getting up Hitler's nose in case it started a war.

Winston was exasperated with Prime Minister Chamberlain's weak-kneed response. He likened him to:

> *An old town clerk looking at European affairs through the wrong end of a municipal drainpipe.*

To be fair to Chamberlain, he wasn't the only one who had misjudged Hitler. No one in Britain wanted another war when they were still recovering from the last one. Many people had lost parents or brothers in the First World War and had no stomach for another fight. They clung to the delusion that what was happening in Europe was nothing to do with them. In 1938 Chamberlain returned from the Munich Conference confident that he'd saved Europe from war.

❧ THE WINSTON WEEKLY ❧
30 September 1938

PEACE IN OUR TIME!

The Prime Minister, Mr Chamberlain, today stepped off a plane waving a piece of paper. The Munich agreement will guarantee 'peace in our time' he told cheering crowds.

Herr Hitler has said that he has nothing but goodwill for Britain.

Winston – the voice of doom – called the Munich agreement 'an awful milestone in our history'. 'Do not suppose this is the end,' he warned. 'This is only the beginning of the reckoning.' Less than a year later he was proved dead right.

THE WINSTON WEEKLY
3 September 1939

WAR IN OUR TIME!

Britain woke up this morning to find itself at war with Germany. Two days ago Hitler's forces marched into Poland. They have since refused to respond to Britain's ultimatum to withdraw. War has been declared.

The Government is assembling a War Cabinet and many people are calling for Winston Churchill to be part of it.

TOLD YOU SO

No sooner had Winston listened to Chamberlain announcing war on the radio than the wail of air-raid sirens split the air. Churchill grabbed a bottle of brandy and a few other 'medical comforts' and went with Clemmie to the shelter at the end of the street.

Throughout the summer of 1939 the calls for

Winston's comeback had become louder and more insistent. The newspapers were full of his name (especially as the *Daily Express* was owned by his old chum, Lord Beaverbrook). An admirer even paid for a large billboard in London which asked the question: 'What price, Winston?' No one really knew the answer, but it kept Churchill's name in the public eye.

Winston's new wave of popularity was based on two things. Firstly during the 1930s he'd become 'a man of the people'. Winston with his hats and cigars, his painting and bricklaying, was a celebrity – a 'character' of the kind the British have always loved. Secondly he'd been proved right all along. For years he'd been warning the government to prepare for war and everyone had scoffed. Now war had come and people saw Winston as the kind of far-sighted leader the country needed.

Reluctantly, Chamberlain was forced to give way to the popular demand to bring back Winston. Churchill was asked if he would accept his old hat at the Admiralty. Naturally he would. At six o' clock on the day when war was declared a three-word message was flashed to all the ships in the Navy: WINSTON IS BACK!

Phoney War

The War started with a deafening silence. During the summer and winter of 1939, very little happened. The air-raid warnings were false alarms. This period became known as the 'Phoney War'. At home the government introduced conscription, calling up men between the ages of 18 and 41 to join the Army. Over a million children were evacuated from the city to live in the country where their parents thought they'd be safer from

German bombs. Everyone was issued with gas masks and went around looking like strange goggle-eyed aliens. Even babies and some family pets had masks.

But the feared poison-gas attacks didn't come and Chamberlain confidently declared, 'Hitler has missed the bus!'

The 'Phoney War' came to an abrupt end in April 1940 when the German Army bulldozed through Denmark and Norway. No one was prepared for the speed of the Nazi onslaught. The German's new method of fighting was called *Blitzkrieg* (lightning war). Previous wars had been fought at a plodding pace with soldiers on foot; now the Germans attacked with regiments of tanks, supported by Stuka dive-bombers swooping down on the enemy from above. Norway and Denmark didn't hold out for long.

The British sent a naval attack to try and help Norway but it was a bungle from start to finish.

The Norwegian shambles had one important result for Britain and for Winston. It brought down Chamberlain's government. Funnily enough, Churchill had been heavily involved but somehow came up smelling of roses. Following the ill-fated Munich agreement, it was the government that people really blamed.

In the time of crisis someone had to take the reins. But who? The choice of Prime Minister came down to two men: the Foreign Secretary, Lord Halifax, or Winston Churchill. The King, Chamberlain and most of the Conservative Party all wanted Lord Halifax. You can guess who became Prime Minister.

WINSTON'S LOST DIARY
10 May 1940

It's a terrible time to become Prime Minister but someone has to do it. And as it turns out old Halifax isn't keen. Who can the country turn to? We need a true leader of men – brave, resourceful, determined, experienced, brilliant. Me, in fact.

Went to bed at 3 am with a strange feeling of calm. It feels like my whole life has been leading up to this moment. It is my Destiny to lead my country. Watch out, Hitler, Winston is in charge!

WINSTON'S WORLD: DAD'S ARMY

As the German Army marched relentlessly on into Holland and Belgium, how did Winston propose to defeat the might of the German Army if it invaded Britain? Apparently with a bunch of old codgers armed with rifles that hadn't been fired since 1918. On 14 May 1940 the call went out for men over 40 to join a local defence force or Home Guard. It was Winston's bright idea to recruit men 'who are full of vigour and experience' but too old to join the regular army. Many of the new recruits – nicknamed Dad's Army – turned up with shotguns, swords or any weapon they thought useful.

If the Germans had ever landed, Dad's Army would have been little use but they did do a valuable job in releasing soldiers from guarding coasts, factories and airfields. By 1943 there would be a staggering 1,750,000 Home Guard volunteers.

Day trip to Dunkirk

In 1940 the Germans looked unstoppable. With Holland and Belgium lost, Britain was pinning its hopes on the French. To hold back the Nazis, the French had built the

Maginot Line – an impressive line of defences stretching all along the French/German border. In the concrete walls heavy artillery guns were mounted in forts. It was just a pity the Germans didn't attack it. Instead they crossed the border through Belgium and came round the side of the Maginot Line. Before long half of France was occupied by the German Army. The remaining French and British troops were forced back into a narrow corridor along the coast at Dunkirk.

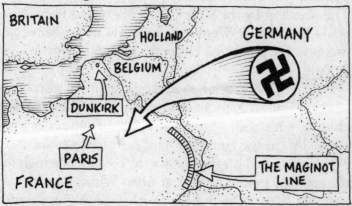

With no way out it looked like curtains for the Allied Army. The British naval ships couldn't get in close enough to the beach for the soldiers to wade out to them. But the Germans hadn't counted on the arrival of an unlikely rescue fleet. Out of the blue came thousands of boats of all shapes and sizes – a mad armada of paddle steamers and pleasure boats called out by Churchill in the country's hour of need. Under the unceasing fire of the Luftwaffe, many ships went down but 338,000 soldiers were rescued from Dunkirk's beaches. The RAF played a key part, fighting the enemy in the sky while heavily outnumbered.

Dunkirk was 'a miracle of deliverance' according to Churchill. But it was still a devastating defeat. Ten days later France surrendered to the Germans. The grim truth had to be faced – Britain was now standing virtually alone. Churchill summed it up in one of his radio broadcasts to the nation – the battle for France was over, the battle for Britain had begun.

Radio Winston

The situation by the summer of 1940 was as bleak as it could be. Most of Western Europe was under Nazi rule and nothing prevented Hitler from turning his guns on Britain.

Privately, some members of the government wondered whether Britain ought to make peace while they had the chance. Churchill scorned any talk of surrender and persuaded the waverers they must fight to the bitter end.

He recognized his first job was to keep morale high in the country. 1940 was the year when Winston became a national hero. How did he do it? By speaking on the radio.

In the 1940s when people wanted to know what was happening they gathered round their wireless set and listened in their millions. The word would go round in pubs, clubs and factories – 'Winston's going to be on' – and everything would stop for the PM's broadcast. For one speech on the 14 July *two-thirds* of the adult population were glued to the radio, listening. Winston's radio broadcasts, read in his solemn booming voice, echoed round the world.

As Edward Murrow said: 'He mobilized the English language and sent it into battle.'

Here are just a few of Winston's famous words.

> *I have nothing to offer but blood, toil, tears and sweat.*

13 May 1940 on becoming PM

> *...if the British Empire and Commonwealth last for a thousand years, men will still say, 'This was their finest hour.'*

18 June 1940 after France had surrendered

> *We shall fight on the beaches. We shall fight on the landing grounds. We shall fight in the fields, and in the streets, we shall fight in the hills. We shall never surrender.*

4 June 1940 after Dunkirk

> *Never in the field of human conflict was so much owed by so many to so few.*

20 August 1940 on the Battle of Britain

One widely repeated story is that Winston never did his famous 'we shall fight on the beaches' speech on the radio. Some claim he made the speech in the Commons and refused to repeat it on the BBC. When the whole country thrilled to the sound of his voice it's said they were actually listening to an actor, Larry the Lamb of Children's Hour, doing a very good impression of Churchill. It's a good story – but not true. Winston didn't much like speaking on radio (he preferred an audience he could see) but he certainly did all his speeches himself.

FIGHTING TALK
A GUIDE TO WWII WORDS

Churchill's famous words will always be remembered, but during the Second World War other words entered the English language and soon became part of everyday conversation.

Blackout – After dark, turn out all lights and cover all windows so the German bombers can't see their target.

Black market – Luxuries like cigarettes and silk stockings were scarce but could be bought illegally through a *spiv* (see below).

Blitz – German campaign of blitz-bombing British cities 1940–41.

Collaborators – Traitors in conquered countries who worked with the Germans.

Doodle-bug – Flying bomb also known as buzz bomb. When the drone of the engine cut out it was time to start praying.

Enigma – German secret code.

Land Army – Women called 'Land Girls' were sent to plough the fields. Some got jobs as rat catchers.

Luftwaffe – German Air Force fighting the RAF (Royal Air Force).

Rationing – Food was scarce and had to be bought with ration coupons so everyone got fair (and measly) shares.

Spiv – Small-time crook who sold stolen or illegal goods on the black market.

Swastika – Symbol of the Nazis. Based on an ancient Hindu sign meaning 'well being'.

Third Reich – The Nazi Empire which would last 1,000 years. Better make that six.

'Our Winnie'

As well as speaking on the radio, the Prime Minister was out and about everywhere, visiting bombed streets in London, dropping into munitions (weapons) factories and inspecting the defences on the coast. Press photographers and film cameras followed him everywhere but he wasn't doing it for their benefit. Winston wanted to see things for himself and to show the people of Britain that he was right behind them. Seeing Winston was a huge boost to public morale. (Hitler was hardly ever seen by ordinary German citizens once the war had started.) For all Winston's privileged background, during the war he succeeded in becoming 'our Winnie', a leader beloved by the whole nation.

Winston had several different styles of dress to suit the occasion. He could be dapper in a suit, military in uniform or plain oddball when he was relaxing. Churchill was never fashionable but he certainly had a style all of his own.

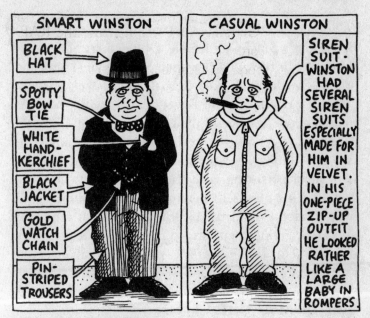

SMART WINSTON	CASUAL WINSTON
BLACK HAT	SIREN SUIT - WINSTON HAD SEVERAL SIREN SUITS ESPECIALLY MADE FOR HIM IN VELVET. IN HIS ONE-PIECE ZIP-UP OUTFIT HE LOOKED RATHER LIKE A LARGE BABY IN ROMPERS.
SPOTTY BOW TIE	
WHITE HAND-KERCHIEF	
BLACK JACKET	
GOLD WATCH CHAIN	
PIN-STRIPED TROUSERS	

The Battle of Britain

Having flattened France, Britain was next on Hitler's shopping list. The invasion was to be called Operation Sealion. There was only one problem with the *Führer's* master plan – and it wasn't overcoming the Home Guard. If the German Army crossed the Channel by barge they would be sitting ducks for the British RAF to swoop down and bomb them.

Hermann Goering, Commander of the Luftwaffe, convinced his leader that the RAF could be put out of action in one great battle for command of the skies. The Battle of Britain began on 13 August, code-named Eagle Day by the Germans (the war was littered with code names). The Luftwaffe were far superior in numbers and seemed bound to win. Worse still, Britain had a severe shortage of trained pilots to keep their planes in the sky.

Throughout the long hot summer of 1940, the Battle of Britain was fought under clear blue skies. The small number of British pilots flew their Spitfires and Hurricanes around the clock, often dazed to the point of exhaustion.

On 5 September the news was worrying: 50 RAF fighter pilots had been killed in a week, but Churchill chose not to report that in the House of Commons. Yet two days later, Goering made a big tactical blunder. Instead of persisting with the battle for the skies, he switched his planes to making massive bombing raids over London. The Battle of Britain ended with the RAF unbowed, giving them breathing space to regroup. For the time being Britain was safe – though it didn't feel that way if you lived in London.

The blasted Blitz

[Hitler] hopes by killing large numbers of civilians, and women and children, that he will terrorize and cow the people of this mighty imperial city…

The bombing of London had begun during the battle for the skies. In September 1940 it intensified. On Sunday 15 September 230 German bombers and 700 fighters crossed the south coast and headed for London. At one point every single British plane was in the air fighting the enemy, with not one left in reserve. Yet the Luftwaffe suffered such heavy losses that they couldn't afford to continue.

Londoners' first warning of an air raid came with the wail of sirens, soon followed by the drone of the bombers overhead. Houses would be in darkness, people used heavy blackout curtains at the windows and turned off all the lights. (Even cars had to black out their headlights to a tiny slit, which, of course, made accidents far more common.)

While the searchlights swept the skies, people took shelter wherever they could.

WINSTON'S WORLD: TAKING SHELTER

1 ANDERSON SHELTER
Outdoor pit covered by a curved roof. People often grew vegetables on top, though they were more in danger from falling marrows than bombs.

2 MORRISON SHELTER
Steel-roofed box kept indoors that was supposed to be able to withstand the collapse of a house.

3 THE UNDERGROUND

Thousands of Londoners sheltered in underground stations. Some had bunk beds but the bad news was there were no toilets. During an air raid you just had to hold on!

4 CAVES

Many Londoners caught the train to Chiselhurst in Kent where they were bats enough to sleep in caves.

5 NO. 10 ANNEXE

If you were the Prime Minister you took shelter in a reinforced steel room in the Board of Trade, with shutters that closed when an air raid began.

The cost of the Blitz was heavy. In the first week of October alone 2,000 people were killed in London and other cities. Although the losses were terrible Hitler was mistaken in thinking that the Blitz would win the war. Winston pointed out that it would take ten years of constant bombing for half of London to be destroyed. To keep up morale he arranged for the anti-aircraft guns to fire noisy blanks when there weren't enough shells in supply. (One local council grumbled that the guns were cracking the toilet bowls in council houses.)

Whenever possible, Winston visited parts of London that had been badly bombed. The reception he got must have touched him deeply.

WINSTON'S LOST DIARY
September 7 1940

Visited an air-raid shelter where 40 people had died the previous night. As I got out of my car I was mobbed by crowds of people. At first I thought they were angry but they were shouting, 'We thought you'd come. We can take it. Give it 'em back!'

I'm not ashamed to say I broke down and blubbed like a baby. As I pushed my way through the crowd to my car a woman called out, 'See? He really cares. He's crying.'

So maybe the waterworks are not such a bad thing after all. The sight of the bombed-out streets is terrible. But am I downhearted? I've never felt more sure of victory.

By mid October the death toll had reached 10,000 in cities such as London, Coventry and Manchester. On one occasion Winston was eating a meal at 10 Downing Street when a bomb fell on nearby Horse Guards Parade. He immediately ordered his butler, cook and servants to leave the food and go to the basement shelter. Just as well. Three minutes later the kitchen was blown up and destroyed altogether.

The Blitz went on into the spring of 1941 – even destroying the Chamber of the House of Commons (though luckily no MPs were making speeches at the time). Yet the real crisis had passed. With the RAF still active in the skies, Hitler was forced to shelve his plans for invading Britain. Operation Sealion was a dead duck. Hitler turned his attention to Greece and Russia. Britain had survived the worst and the time was coming when it could start to bite back.

WINSTON AND THE BIG THREE

In the early years of the war Britain had looked isolated and vulnerable, holding on by the skin of its teeth while one by one the other nations of Europe were swallowed up by the German advance.

1941 was the year the tide began to turn. Up until now all Winston had to throw at Hitler were brave words and the Home Guard changing the signposts so that invading Nazis would lose their way.

Battle of the Atlantic

At sea, a battle for survival was being waged. Even if Hitler couldn't invade Britain, he still had a masterplan up his sleeve to put his enemy out of the war:

> # Mein brilliant masterplan by A Hitler
>
> 1 Britain is an island –
>   (Ha ha! You think I hadn't noticed?)
> 2 So it relies on ships to bring in food and supplies
> 3 Mein plan is simple – we cut off the supply line by sinking the ships
> 4 And the British dogs will be starved into surrender!
>
> Heil me!

The Battle of the Atlantic was the longest battle of the Second World War and the one that worried Winston most. The menace to the merchant ships crossing the Atlantic from America was silent and deadly. They were called German U-boats.

The U stood for *Unterseeboot* (undersea boat) and each German submarine was called U followed by its number.

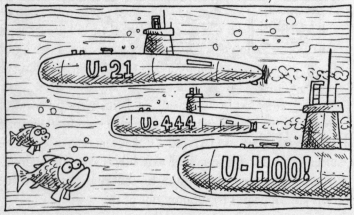

Churchill was very clear that enemy submarines should always be called U-boats.

The term submarine is to be reserved for Allied underwater vessels. U-boats are those dastardly villains who sink our ships, while submarines are those gallant and noble craft which sink theirs.

The tactics of the U-boats were deadly and effective. They would form a line like a long underwater net across the Atlantic, waiting for any convoys of ships to pass. Once a merchant ship was sighted, the U-boats struck without warning – forming a wolf pack that closed in under cover of night.

In the early years of the war the German U-boats were very effective. Their submariners called it the 'happy time' though it wasn't much fun if you were on a British merchant ship crossing the Atlantic. Three million tons of Allied shipping was sunk in the last six months of 1940 alone. When one of Winston's staff called the latest attack 'distressing' he replied. *'Distressing!* It's terrifying. If it goes on it will be the end of us!'

Fortunately as the war went on Britain found ways to combat the U-boat menace. Corvettes – small mobile warships – were used to escort the convoys across the dangerous seas. These were eventually backed up by long-range aircraft that could fly over the Atlantic and force enemy submarines to submerge.

The third main weapon against the U-boats was intelligence (intelligence meant top-secret information, not using your brain). In May 1941 the Royal Navy made a hugely important breakthrough when they sighted a U-boat off Greenland.

The Enigma code

The Enigma code was used by the Germans to pass messages to their armed forces on land, sea and in the air. The signals were sent by radio but didn't make any sense, unless you knew the key to the fiendishly difficult code. The Enigma machine and the code books from captured U-boat 110 were taken to Churchill's top-secret team of code-breakers at Bletchley (see page 150). The information they provided played a key part in solving the puzzle of Enigma and winning the Battle of the Atlantic. After 1941 British convoys often knew the position of the enemy wolf packs hunting for them. The Germans considered their Enigma code unbreakable. It would have horrified them to know that Churchill's Secret Service was not only intercepting their messages, but was also able to read them.

The Battle of the Atlantic reached its climax in 1943 when 200 U-boats were in operation and the Allies destroyed almost half of them in the first six months of the year. By that May, Admiral Donitz, the German commander, knew his subs were sunk and the U-boat attacks were called off. The Allies had won perhaps the most important battle they would wage.

But that's getting ahead a bit. At the end of 1941 an event on the little known Hawaiian island of Oahu changed the course of the war.

THE WINSTON WEEKLY
8 December 1941

PEARL HARBOR ATTACKED!

At 7.55 am yesterday morning the skies over Pearl Harbor swarmed with 200 Japanese dive bombers and fighter planes. Below them 70 American warships were moored in the large natural harbour on Oahu Island. Since it was a Sunday most of their crews were taking a day off and the harbour was poorly defended.

For an hour and a half the Japanese bombers, launched secretly from nearby aircraft carriers, lit up the skies with explosions. By the time they wheeled away they had totally destroyed the American fleet, leaving 2,000 Americans dead. Before the USA has even entered the war, Japan has struck a crippling blow to its sea power.

On the face of it, Pearl Harbor was a disaster. So why did Churchill find some crumbs of hope in the terrible news? Because the Japanese attack made certain that America would enter the war. The tide had turned at last and Churchill felt confident that, with the help of American troops, Hitler would eventually be defeated.

Hitler followed Pearl Harbor by declaring war on America four days later.

Meanwhile Germany had invaded Russia. Back in 1812 another dictator called Napoleon Bonaparte found his plans to conquer Europe frozen out by the Russian winter. Was Adolf Hitler about to make the same mistake?

The Big Three

The attack on Pearl Harbor and Hitler's invasion of Russia brought together Britain, USA and Russia to form the Allies – united against Germany and its friends Japan and Italy. (Or the Axis of Evil as Churchill liked to call them.)

War makes strange bedfellows. While America and Britain were on good terms, Churchill hated Stalin's cruel dictatorship in Russia. In many ways Stalin was as big a monster as Hitler. He ruled by fear and anyone who opposed him mysteriously 'disappeared'. Until Hitler attacked Russia in 1941 Stalin was perfectly prepared to let the Nazis take over Western Europe, leaving Russia to gobble up the east. The leaders, known as the Big Three, worked together but Churchill never totally trusted Stalin.

In contrast he was on good terms with Roosevelt, even if they didn't always see eye to eye. Roosevelt once walked in on Churchill when he was emerging from the bath, stark naked. Never lost for words, Churchill said:

The Prime Minister of Britain has nothing to hide from the President of the United States.

THE BIG THREE

WINSTON CHURCHILL - BRITISH PRIME MINISTER
APPEARANCE: LARGE BALD BABY
NICKNAME: WINNIE
WINSTON ON WINSTON:
'A small lion walking between a great Russian bear and a great American elephant'.

FRANKLIN D ROOSEVELT - PRESIDENT OF THE UNITED STATES
APPEARANCE: ROOSEVELT HAD POLIO AS A CHILD AND SPENT MUCH OF HIS LIFE IN A WHEELCHAIR.
NICKNAME: FDR
SAD FACT: ROOSEVELT DIED ONLY WEEKS BEFORE GERMANY SURRENDERED
ROOSEVELT ON WINSTON: 'Churchill has a hundred ideas a day, of which four are good ideas.'

JOE STALIN – PREMIER OF RUSSIA

APPEARANCE: NOT-SO-CUDDLY BEAR
NICKNAME: UNCLE JOE
MAD FACT: IF ANY RUSSIAN SOLDIERS WERE CAPTURED BY THE NAZIS THEY WERE BRANDED AS TRAITORS.
WINSTON ON STALIN: HE ONCE PROPOSED A TOAST 'To Premier Stalin whose conduct of foreign policy manifests a desire for peace', -ADDING IN A LOW VOICE: 'A piece of Poland, a piece of Czechoslovakia...'

Ssh! Top secret!

By 1942 the war was being fought all across the world. Meanwhile in Britain, another war was being waged secretly in Bletchley Park, Bedfordshire. The men and women working at Bletchley were Winston's team of top code-breakers whose job was to crack the enemy's coded messages. Winston called his team of Bletchley boffins:

My geese that laid the Golden Eggs and never cackled.

Only a handful of outsiders knew the truth about Bletchley Park (code-named Station X). One of them was Group Captain Fred Winterbotham, who Churchill made his liason officer. Winterbotham's job was to sift through the decoded messages each day and send anything important to MI6 – the Military Intelligence (or Secret Service). Once the messages had been read they were locked in a box and carried down the road by hand to 10 Downing Street where they were handed to the Prime Minister. Only Winston had a key to open the top-secret box.

Almost 9,000 people worked at Bletchley during the war and they were an odd bunch of scientists, boffins and eggheads. Their living quarters were primitive wooden army huts and at times the staff got on each other's nerves in the cramped conditions.

In the late summer of 1941 unrest among the staff got so bad that Winston paid a personal visit. Typically he found an original solution to the problem of low staff morale. When Churchill asked what recreational facilities there were, he was told 'none at all'. Winston pointed to an area that was set aside for a car park and ordered that it should be turned into tennis courts. Before long, Bletchley Park gained the only tennis courts in Britain built by order of the Prime Minister.

Many experts agree that the Bletchley code-breakers played a key role in the Allied victory of 1945 and may even have shortened the war by two years. The boffins of Station X had another claim to fame too – they created the world's first computer nicknamed Colossus. By the end of the war there were ten Colossus computers at work every hour of the day and night, breaking the enemy's coded messages.

Colossus didn't look much like today's computers. Each one was almost 5 metres long, 3.5 metres wide and 2.5 metres high, with up to 2,500 valves. Today a matchbox-sized microchip can deal with the same amount of information!

AND WE CALL THIS OUR POCKET COMPUTER!

And how were recruits found for Churchill's top team of code-breakers?

By a rather puzzling method…

The strange case of Stanley Sedgewick

Stanley Sedgewick liked to do crosswords. As an accountancy manager he hadn't yet been called up to the Army. Every day Stanley travelled to his job in London and did the *Daily Telegraph* crossword to pass the train journey. At the end of 1941, when the *Telegraph* published their 5,000th crossword, Stanley spotted an intriguing letter in the paper. It was from a Mr W A J Gavin of the Eccentric Club who said he would donate £100 to the Minesweepers Fund if anyone could solve the *Telegraph* crossword in under 12 minutes. For a crossword king like Stanley the challenge was too good to resist.

The following January, Stanley found himself with 24 other crossword fans at the offices of the *Telegraph*. Under the eyes of a panel and a timekeeper each challenger was handed the crossword to compete. The first person to finish did it in 6 minutes, 3.5 seconds. Sadly they were disqualified for a spelling mistake. Four other people completed the puzzle within the time limit. When the 12-minute bell rang Stanley kicked himself – he was just one word short of finishing. After tea in the chairman's dining room he went home and thought little more about it.

To Stanley's surprise, shortly after he got a letter from a Colonel Nichols of Military Intelligence asking him to come to an interview. Stanley's talent with solving clues had got him recruited for Station X. After training in spy school, he worked at Bletchley on German weather codes to help Bomber Command (see below). It was only after the war that he learnt how vital his work had been.

Bomber Command

While the secret battle of spying was going on, the battle for the air raged over Germany.

As early as 1940 Churchill felt, 'the Navy can lose us the war but only the air force can win it.' Britain's only way of striking back at Hitler for much of the war was by launching massive bombing raids on Germany.

The aim of Bomber Command was to damage Germany's war output and shatter the morale of the German people. It was a half-baked idea since the Blitz only strengthened the determination of the British.

On 30 May 1942, Bomber Harris, Commander in Chief, launched his first 'thousand-bomber raid' on Cologne. By the following year 40,000 Germans had died in the city – more than in Britain during the entire war. Winston privately had his doubts about Bomber Command and once, when watching a film of German cities burning, burst out, 'Are we beasts? Are we taking this too far?'

All work and no play?

Meanwhile Winston, now in his late sixties, took on a superhuman workload. Often he worked until two in the morning – fine for him but tough on his staff who weren't allowed a cat nap in the afternoon. Winston was always on the go and rarely got the chance to visit his beloved Chartwell. Most of the time he flitted between Parliament, Downing Street, Chequers (the PM's country retreat) and the mansion at Ditchley, Oxfordshire, owned by the MP Ronald Tree. His private secretaries hardly ever knew where he was going to turn up next. One of them once wrote his own spoof note from the PM which gives an idea of the kind of demands Winston made.

Action This Day
Pray let six new offices be fitted for my use in Selfridge's, Lambeth Palace, Stanmore, Tooting Bec, the Palladium and Mile End Road. I will inform you at six each evening at which office I shall dine, work and sleep. Accommodation will be required for Mrs Churchill, two shorthand writers, three secretaries and Nelson (the cat). There should be shelter for all, and a place for me to watch air raids from the roof.

WSC

At least Churchill was a difficult target for German bombs, he never kept still long enough to be hit.

Despite his heavy workload, Winston never forgot to make time for play. His great loves were food, champagne, good company and films – and even in war time he squeezed in all four.

The silver screen

Winston had been a film fan since the 1920s when he often went to the cinema. During the war it was less easy for the Prime Minister to sneak into a cinema without attracting attention, but that didn't stop him. Churchill simply had a projector installed at Chequers or Ditchley so he could have his own private cinema. Like Hitler and Stalin, Winnie's favourite time for watching films was after midnight, when he could sit in a cloud of cigar smoke and lose himself after a hard day's work.

During the summer of 1941 he watched a dozen films including comedies such as *Saps at Sea* with Laurel and Hardy and a Donald Duck and Goofy film. Thrillers such as *High Sierra* starring Humphrey Bogart, made him chuckle. When the film ended with the dead baddie rolling down a rocky mountainside, Churchill remarked, 'And a good time was had by all!'

Winston's pet poodle Rufus often used to sit on his master's lap while they watched the film. Once, when a scene in *Oliver* showed the evil Bill Sykes drowning his dog, Churchill quickly put a hand over his pet's eyes.

Winston's favourite films were romantic and heroic, just like him. It is said that he watched the film about Lord Nelson, *Lady Hamilton*, 17 times and the story always moved him to tears. Then again, a lot of things moved Winston to tears.

Away from the make-believe of films, there were some thrilling stories unfolding in the war itself. By 1942–43 Hitler's all-conquering Army was starting to suffer its first major setbacks.

Both battles were a serious blow to Hitler's plans. At the first battle of El Alamein, in Northern Egypt, the Allied Army had finally halted the German advance across North Africa. In the return match, Montgomery and his men drove the Panzer troops all the way back to

Tunisia. Before El Alamein, as Churchill pointed out, the Allies had hardly won a battle, afterwards they never lost one.

In Russia, it was a similar story. Germany had swept across the country until they reached the streets of Stalingrad. There the Russian Army had reinforcements who surrounded the Germans, encircling them on all sides. Cut off from food supplies and frozen by the Russian snow, the Germans tried desperately to break out but were forced to surrender. A staggering 800,000 of them died in the battle.

V FOR VICTORY

In 1943 there were three attempts to bump off Hitler. (Amazingly there were six attempts to kill Hitler altogether – and every one of them was bungled .)

It seemed if Hitler was going to be stopped it would have to be done the hard way – with an invasion of Europe by the Allies. Stalin had been urging Britain to get on with it for a long time. Roosevelt and the Americans were equally keen to launch an assault on Europe as early as 1942. Only Churchill dragged his feet. After the near disaster of Dunkirk he was worried about landing an army on the French coast again. But this time he was outvoted and plans for Operation Overlord started to take shape.

Even at 66 years old Winston – the old warhorse – hadn't changed a bit. He was desperate to be at the head of the Allied invasion when it set foot on French soil. In fact this was the one time Churchill had a real argument with the King, as they both wanted to go. In the end Winston was forced to listen to reason and stay at home.

Surprise, surprise

By the spring of 1944 the plans for D-day were in place.
An army of almost one and a half million soldiers had
massed in Britain, coming from as far afield as Canada,
the USA, Australia, Africa and India.

The utmost secrecy was vital. The Germans knew an
invasion was coming (a whopping great army gathering
across the Channel was a little bit obvious). But what
they didn't know was where or when. An invasion of
Europe was a risky business and Winston was worried
about it. Not only did the Allies have to get their army
across the sea, they then had to land them on the French
coast right under the noses of the Nazis. If the plan was
going to succeed the element of surprise was vital. If
Winston had kept a diary it would have been even more
secret than usual.

WINSTON'S LOST DIARY

3 June 1945

Two days until Overlord or you-know-
what as I like to call it. The plan is to
tow our dear old Mulberry across the
Channel to help speed up the whole
process of unloading.

Then it's the Americans for Utah and
Omaha and our lads for Gold, Juno and
Sword. The bombers will be pounding

the enemy all along the coast while Neptune rules the sea.

It's all quite clear – what can go wrong?

<u>5 June</u>

Disaster! Overlord's been put back by 24 hours. Trust the British weather to turn nasty just when you don't need it!

If you can't make head or tail of this, it's not surprising. Churchill would have used code-names so that he didn't give away any secrets to sneaky German spies. Here are the secret codes to help you make sense of the above.

OPERATION OVERLORD – The code-name for the entire D-day invasion.

MULBERRY – The name for two floating concrete harbours that the Allies actually towed across the Channel. Once they were sunk in position on the coast, the tanks and armoured vehicles could be unloaded onto them, saving time.

UTAH and OMAHA, GOLD, JUNO and SWORD – The five Normandy beaches where the invading army would land.

NEPTUNE – Code-name for the naval part of the invasion.

TOP SECRET!

As well as all the secrecy, the Allies had a few fiendishly clever tricks up their sleeves to make sure that Operation Overlord was a success.

1 Blow-up tanks – It sounds like a load of hot air but the Allies actually landed some inflatable tanks near Calais. The idea was to fool the enemy into thinking the invasion was taking place up the coast. When the Nazis fired on them they must have gone off with a bang.

2 Holiday snaps – As early as 1942 an appeal was made on BBC radio for people to loan their holiday photos of the Normandy coast to military intelligence. Daft as it sounds, holiday snaps were used to help plan the invasion.

3 Carrier pigeons – How did details of the D-day landings get back to HQ in Britain? Via a carrier pigeon called Gustav, who was later awarded the Dickin medal for bravery.

COO, THANKS!

Despite all the careful planning, the D-day invasion could have gone badly wrong if the Nazis had been more prepared. Hitler had put his finest commander, General Rommel, in charge of defending the French coast and Rommel had ringed the coast with gun forts, underwater obstacles and tank traps. Yet as dawn broke on 6 June and the invasion got underway, Hitler's army was having a bit of an off day. The *Führer* himself was asleep and nobody dared to wake him until late morning, when it was a bit late. Meanwhile General Rommel was away on a day trip to Ulm in Germany. What was he doing so far from the action? It was his wife's birthday.

As for Winston himself, he was pacing his Map Room in London, anxiously waiting for news of the invasion. As it turned out the news was better than Churchill could have hoped for. On the first day 156,000 Allied troops were landed on the Normandy beaches. The surprise invasion had worked and although around 10,000 men were lost in the fierce fighting, Churchill had feared it would be much worse. Much of the success of D-day and the victories that followed was thanks to the brilliance of the Allied generals in command.

Montgomery

Nickname:	Monty
What did he do?	Beat Rommel in North Africa and led the British forces on D-day.
General fact:	Monty had two pet dogs he called Hitler and Rommel.
Winston's view:	'In defeat unbeatable; in victory, unbearable.'

Montgomery

Eisenhower

Nickname:	Ike
What did he do?	Supreme Commander of the D-day invasion.
General Fact:	Eisenhower was such a hit that he later became President of America.

Eisenhower

Patton

Nickname:	Old Blood and Guts (because he was a tough old boot).
What did he do?	Led the US 3rd army as it fought across France and into Germany.
General Fact:	Patton was a Texan who liked to wear big boots and carry a pair of ivory-handled revolvers. No one with any sense called him a cowboy.

General Patton

Six days after the invasion, Winston finally got his wish and was taken to Normandy on a destroyer ship. When he landed he couldn't resist sending a postcard to President Roosevelt with a short message.

165

Victory V

Wherever he went in Britain, Italy or France, Winston never failed to salute the troops with his two-fingered victory salute. Some of his staff didn't like it, but that never stopped Winston from using it whenever possible.

As early as 1941 the BBC took up the V for Victory campaign and broadcast the slogan abroad. V happened to be the first letter of the French word for victory and the Dutch word for freedom. The V for Victory slogan spread through Europe, and Resistance fighters in France were soon painting a V on public buildings as mark of defiance. Only the Nazi Minister Goebbels failed to understand the sign. He placed a massive V sign on the Eiffel Tower, not realizing that to the rest of Paris it meant: 'Down with Hitler!'

Deadly doodlebugs

Back home in Britain the war wasn't quite over yet. Hitler was convinced he'd found a secret weapon that could still win the war for Germany. It was called the doodlebug. He'd tried blitzing the Brits before in 1940–41, but this time he had something new – a bomb called the V1. The flying bombs were planes without pilots and created panic in London, Kent and Sussex. They flew overhead at a speed of 600 km/h, making a droning noise like an angry bee. (They were also known as buzz bombs.) When the droning stopped they'd run out of fuel, which was the time to start panicking since the bomb was about to fall.

In the first week of raids, 700 flying V1 bombs were sent over and 200 were shot down by anti-aircraft guns or British fighter planes. The flying bombs were difficult to combat. RAF Spitfires sometimes fired on them but they also found that if they flew in close and tipped up the doodlebug's wing, the bomb spiralled out of control.

Before the war was over the deadly doodlebugs killed 6,000 people and caused another wave of evacuation from London. Churchill himself was once dictating a telegram to Roosevelt in his Map Room when he broke off to mention that a flying bomb was approaching. Later in the telegram he added, 'Bomb has fallen some way off.'

HE'S RIGHT! IT FELL OVER HERE!

In September 1944 the V1 was replaced by the V2 which was even worse because it gave no warning sound at all. Churchill was so worried by the threat of the doodlebugs that he even considered 'mustard gas' attacks on Germany.

Clemmie's war

Winston continued to visit areas of London that had been worst hit by the bombs. On these visits, Clemmie often accompanied him, knowing it was the only way to get him home to bed before nightfall.

The war was tough for Clemmie. Winston was often away for days at a time and didn't bother about his own safety. When bombs were falling over London he liked to watch from his balcony rather than take cover.

It was Clemmie who worked with Lord Beaverbrook on turning London underground stations into giant air-raid shelters during the Blitz, when two million bunks were set up along the platforms.

SORRY TO BOTHER YOU, MRS C, BUT WE'VE ONLY GOT ONE MILLION NINE HUNDRED AND EIGHTY THREE PILLOWS...

She said she never really thought about life after the war. Winston was 70 and she thought he would die when it was over.

...we are putting all we have into this war, and it will take all we have.

One story illustrates the kind of sacrifices she had to make. On Christmas Eve 1943, she had all the family together at Chequers and a special Christmas tree had arrived as a present from President Roosevelt. The grandchildren gathered round it, eager to see it lit. Just then a telegram arrived from Athens saying that British troops in Greece were under severe attack. Typically

Winston decided to leave London on a plane that night, missing the lighting of the tree and Christmas lunch the next day. The war always came first and Clemmie and the family a poor second.

Bye bye, Hitler

The doodlebug terror was Hitler's last shot at winning the war. From D-day onwards the Allied armies pushed further across France and into Germany itself. By April 1945 the liberating army had fought its way into Hitler's last stronghold – the city of Berlin. From Russia the Red Army had advanced across Germany from the east and also reached Berlin. It was clear the war was over.

As Hitler's army crumbled all around him, where was the power-crazy painter who had started it all? He was in a concrete bunker in the heart of Berlin. Unable to accept that his plans for world domination were over, he seemed to be living his last hours in a dream. He played with models of Nazi buildings he was going to build after the war was over. When the sound of the approaching guns got close, he married his long-time mistress, Eva Braun, in a secret ceremony. Shortly afterwards they shot themselves in a pact to die together. Churchill was told the news while dining at 10 Downing Street.

Grimmer news emerged as the Allied troops reached the concentration camps and sent back horrific photos of the dead and starving victims. Six million people had died in the Nazi camps.

Hang out the flags

On 7 May 1945 the Germans finally surrendered and on the following day victory celebrations were held all over

Britain. Winston's famous V for Victory salute had at last come true. The celebrations were called VE day – standing for Victory in Europe. (Japan was still stubbornly carrying on the war in the east.)

People everywhere rushed out to buy flags and decorations for one great almighty party. In many ways it was Winston's finest hour when the whole country thanked him for leading them to victory.

THE WINSTON WEEKLY
8 May 1945

IT'S OVER! VICTORY IN EUROPE!

Britain celebrated wildly today as war in Europe came to an end. Victory in Europe was celebrated with street parties, flag-waving, bonfires, fireworks and music.

Prime Minister, Winston Churchill, the hero of the hour, lunched with the King at Buckingham Palace and then broadcast to the nation on the BBC.

As he was driven to the House of Commons, he was besieged by huge crowds cheering and waving their hats. 'This is your victory,' Mr Churchill told them. 'No, it's yours!' they roared back. The Prime Minister later stood on the balcony of the Ministry of Health and told the crowds, 'In all our long history we have never seen a day like this... God bless you all.'

As the celebrations went on into the night, Winston returned to his office to work through a stack of telegrams six inches high. One of them, from Anthony Eden, a future Prime Minister, summed up the feelings of most people:

It is you who have led, uplifted and inspired us throughout the worst days. Without you this day could not have been.

Churchill hadn't always been right during the war. He was sometimes difficult, often stubborn and frequently drove his generals up the wall and round the bend.

In public he was always confident and smiling, in private he could be a bad-tempered old grump. Yet Hitler couldn't have been defeated without him. Winston's great achievement was to rally his country in its darkest hour when the Nazis threatened to conquer all of Europe. He never admitted defeat and his stirring speeches broadcast to the nation, made him a hero around the world. Winnie with his bulldog spirit and defiant victory salute captured the heart of the nation.

And the winner is...

The war wasn't fully over until America dropped the atom bomb on Japan.

Japan, faced with a weapon that could destroy an entire city, surrendered soon after.

Back in Britain Winston was looking forward to being Prime Minister of a country at peace. As it turned out the public had other ideas.

In the General Election campaign of 1945 Winston was cheered wherever he went. He thought it impossible that 'the man who won the war' wouldn't be trusted with the peace. But the choice wasn't for or against Churchill it was between the Labour Party and the Conservative Party. Labour seemed to have a much clearer idea of how they were going to rebuild Britain after the war. Their 'socialist' ideas included:

• 'nationalizing' the railways, coal mines, gas and electricity
• creating a National Health Service so that everyone was entitled to free health care
• a massive building programme to create new houses.

Churchill's response was a blunder. He said that Attlee's socialism would require 'some sort of Gestapo' to make it work. It was a daft comment and it backfired. People remembered the Conservatives as the party that tried to bargain with Hitler. They lost the election, with Labour winning by a landslide 393 seats to 197. Churchill came back from negotiating with the Americans and Russians to find he was out in the cold.

Clemmie told him that maybe it was a blessing in disguise. If so, it was a very good disguise, replied a gloomy Winston.

Past his 70th birthday, surely it was time for the Grand Old Man to retire, people said. But Winnie wasn't the retiring type. Giving in, calling it a day, admitting defeat – these were phrases that just weren't part of his vocabulary. There was still life in the old dog yet, even if everyone else thought he was barking.

WINSTON'S LAST HOORAY

After the war, Winston enjoyed being a worldwide celebrity, known and recognized everywhere. True, he was no longer Prime Minister, but that didn't stop him making speeches and hogging all the headlines. Winston in old age turned himself into the star of his own film. His hats, his uniforms, his velvet boiler suits, big cigars and habit of crying in public – made him instantly recognizable and as British as fish and chips.

It's more than likely that Winston was well aware he was playing a part and knew what was expected of him. When he visited America in 1946, for instance, he was to be driven through the streets of Fulton, Missouri, so the crowds could cheer him. Churchill refused to begin the procession until someone found a match to light his cigar. His public expected him to be smoking a big fat cigar and that's exactly what he would give them.

In the same way, he kept up his habit of 'making an entrance' on big occasions. The biggest of these was the wedding of Princess Elizabeth (soon to be the next queen) at Westminster Abbey in 1947. The star of the show was meant to be the royal bride, but Winston managed to arrive late so that everyone could give him a standing ovation.

Even in old age Winston loved the limelight and was only happy when he was the centre of attention.

After the hectic war years, Winston hated not being in power and was determined to have one more shot at being Prime Minister.

As Leader of the Opposition, he only turned up for the big occasions in Parliament and annoyed members of his party by frequently popping off on his travels. During his trip to America he made a speech about the 'Iron Curtain' which had fallen across Europe dividing Russia and Eastern Europe from the west. While Hitler was a threat, Russia fought alongside the Allies, but once the war ended Stalin simply took over eastern countries such as Poland and Czechoslovakia.

Churchill's 'Iron Curtain' speech went down like a lead balloon but once again he was right – a new war of secrecy and mistrust was beginning between America and Russia, which became known as the 'Cold War'.

Books and big bucks

One thing that changed in the twilight years was that for the first time in his life, Winston was rich. One reason for this was that he'd gone back to writing books. Being Winston, he felt he was the best qualified person to write a history of the Second World War telling the real story. Winston felt it was such a big story that he produced six huge volumes.

For his biggest book yet he received a fat advance of £550,000 from the *Daily Telegraph* and a million dollars for his memoirs appearing in *Life* magazine.

Churchill's study was his writing room. On his large table rested porcelain busts of Napoleon and Nelson, two of his great war heroes. His books were organized like a military campaign with a team of researchers as Churchill's foot soldiers. 'Camps were set up; intelligence gathered, reports compiled,' said Winston. When the material was gathered, he would give it the famous Churchillian style – setting out the story in his heroic language. Favourite Churchill words were:

VAST, GRIM, FEARSOME, IMMENSE, SOLID, COURAGE, FORMIDABLE.

In the past his scribbling had got him out of debt, now it meant he could live out his old age in style. Churchill bought racehorses and planned yet more rebuilding of his beloved house at Chartwell. He didn't have to worry about the cost as his home was bought for the nation by the National Trust. Clemmie and Winston could carry on living there as long as they liked.

But the story of Winston's life isn't quite over – it has one final episode left.

In 1951 he got his wish of becoming Prime Minister once again. At the staggering age of 76 Winnie was back in power, after the Conservatives narrowly won the General Election.

Not everyone was pleased. Many of Churchill's own party secretly thought it was time for the Grand Old Man to leave the stage and let a younger man take over. But not even Clemmie dared to suggest the idea. Power was the air Winston lived and breathed, without it he was bored and depressed.

During his second stint as Prime Minister it was true he wasn't half the man he used to be.

GOING A BIT DEAF, BUT REFUSES TO WEAR A HEARING AID

TIRES EASILY

WALKING CANE

STILL ON THE PORKY SIDE

BRITISH BULLDOG EXPRESSION

WINSTON – 76 NOT OUT

Rumours whispered that the old man was going ga-ga and could no longer follow the business of a Prime Minister. It wasn't true. Churchill tired more easily and talked so much that the rest of his Cabinet couldn't get a word in edgeways, but that was nothing new. His timetable hadn't changed much either. Breakfast at nine would be taken with a whisky and soda. He would still stay in bed most of the morning reading his papers and dictating letters to his secretaries.

If ministers came to 10 Downing Street for meetings they had to share them with Rufus the poodle and Toby the budgerigar. This sometimes had embarrassing results. Once, after a visit from the Chancellor of the Exchequer, Rab Butler, one of Winston's secretaries reported:

Halfway through his second term as Prime Minister, Winston's health took an alarming nosedive. It happened at the end of a large dinner at Downing Street for the Prime Minister of Italy. Churchill had just made a witty speech, but as his guests were leaving he seemed to have trouble standing up. He was helped to a chair and the guests were told he was over-tired. The truth was he'd suffered a serious stroke. Almost anyone else would have taken to their bed but Winston refused to be beaten. The next day he sat through a Cabinet meeting as usual, and no one seemed to notice that the PM was unusually quiet and pale, with his mouth not quite under control.

None of the newspapers were told about the Prime Minister's stroke and within months Winston had made an amazing recovery. Nevertheless it increased the feeling that Churchill would have to go sooner or later. Most of the Government thought sooner; but Winston preferred later.

Measly meals

Winston's second reign as Prime Minister could hardly be as eventful as the first, since there was no world war to fight. Winston preferred to look at the big picture – relations with America and the problem of Russia – leaving small matters to other people. He did keep his election promise of building 300,000 new houses and interfered in subjects that mattered to him. Food was one subject close to his heart and he was bothered that six years after the War, there were still shortages. Most basic foods were still 'rationed' which meant each person was allowed a measly amount a week. Imagine surviving on the following for a whole seven days:

Churchill was puzzled by these figures and asked for a model of the food to be laid out on a dish so he could see exactly what it looked like. It was duly brought and the Prime Minister looked with satisfaction at the neat piles of sugar, tea, cheese and bacon.

Winston still ate grouse or partridge for breakfast and had no idea how ordinary people lived. He suggested they should eat pork. When this was rejected, he strongly supported bringing back the banana. The yellow peril was hardly seen in 1951.

Food shortages didn't end overnight but gradually supplies improved. By 1953 Winston was able to announce an end to the rationing of really vital foods like…

The Prime Minister, meanwhile, continued to enjoy the best of everything. His cook at 10 Downing Street during the 1940s and 1950s was Georgina Landemere – who later published her recipes from Number 10. In case you've ever wanted to eat like Britain's greatest leader, here's one of the recipes Churchill enjoyed.

BOODLE'S ORANGE FOOL

Note: Boodles was an exclusive London
lunch club which Churchill was allowed to
join after the war. (Most members were
royalty.)

A Fool is an idiot, obviously - but also a
dessert made of whipped cream and
crushed fruit. Maybe the name comes
from the French word 'fouler' - to crush -
or perhaps some fool just made it up.

Ingredients:
6 sponge cakes
4 oranges - grate two, juice all four
2 lemons, grate one, juice both
16 oz pint of cream
one quarter of a cup of sugar

Cut up the sponge cakes lengthways into
slices and put in a glass dish.
In a bowl put the grated rind of one lemon
and two oranges and all the fruit juice.
Mix with the cream and sugar.
Pour the mixture over the sponge cakes
and leave for six hours. (Read one of
Winston's books.)

Serve cold.

In 1954, Churchill reached the milestone of his 80th birthday. In his honour the MPs kindly clubbed together to buy him a birthday present – a portrait of himself painted by the famous artist Graham Sutherland. Winston did his best to look grateful – which wasn't easy since he hated the picture as soon as he set eyes on it. 'Filthy' was his verdict. Clemmie had to agree that it made him look like a fat old monster. Funnily enough the painting was never hung at Chartwell and mysteriously disappeared. What could have happened to it?

Leaving the stage

For Winston the party was finally over and he couldn't put off retirement any longer. The next Tory Prime Minister, Anthony Eden, had been waiting impatiently in the wings for some time. Everyone thought Winston should go and though he tried to find reasons to stay on, he had to make his exit. On 5 April 1955 he took his last Cabinet meeting. As he left the room, someone reminded him that he embodied almost 60 years of British history.

It was true. Churchill had played a major role in the General Strike, the crisis of King Edward's abdication and two world wars. He was still there when the young Queen Elizabeth was crowned. His country had heaped him with so many honours he was weighed down with medals and gowns. In 1953 he accepted the Order of the Garter and became known as Sir Winston (though Clemmie wanted them both to remain plain Mr and Mrs Churchill). The same year he was awarded the Nobel Prize for Literature for his mastery of historical writing and defence of human values. '£12,000 free of tax. Not so bad!' Winston told Clemmie. There was even the chance that Churchill would be made a duke, except that dukes were usually royalty and what would Winston be duke of? 'Duke of Chartwell and Randolph would be Marquess of Toodledo,' joked Winston.

The Queen was assured Churchill would refuse the title and therefore (in the odd way of royalty) offered it to him anyway. When it came to the meeting, Winston was so touched by the young Queen's charm and kindness that he almost changed his mind and accepted!

WINSTON RETIRED

What was a man like Winston to do if he retired? In fact, he remained an MP until 1964, but he did little but keep his seat warm in the House of Commons. Having no real influence only made him bored and depressed. Winston himself told a friend:

I feel like an aeroplane at the end of its flight, in the dusk, with the petrol running out, looking for a safe landing.

Winston's last years were a little sad. The fuel of his superhuman energy was at last running low. He became more and more silent. He liked to indulge his new passion for racing – one of his racehorses won 13 races – and still kept up painting and writing.

Much of the time he spent abroad, sunning himself with the rich on the French Riviera.

Churchill often stayed at the houses of his rich friends – Beaverbrook's or Lord Rothemere's villa, or the yacht of the millionaire Aristotle Onassis.

In his sunset years, Winston was treated like royalty and travelled in style. If you lent Winston your villa, he often arrived with his two daughters, Mary and Diana, Diana's husband, two secretaries, his personal valet and writing assistants. The amount of luggage he needed was colossal. On a trip to Marrakech in 1951 the family had over 100 pieces of luggage.

While his father was still alive, Randolph started on the huge task of writing Winston's biography. The story of his life would run to at least five volumes, naturally – and a lot of it would be in the great man's own words. Churchill had his own doubts about whether Randolph was up to the task and, as it turned out, his son completed only two volumes before he died. One of Churchill's writing team, Martin Gilbert, completed six more books in what became probably the biggest biography in history. Churchill was a big man in every way and he'd lived a long life. There were over 16 books alone of his letters, memos and diary extracts.

Amazingly the Grand Old Man lived on into the 1960s. Born in the reign of Queen Victoria, he lived long enough to hear The Beatles. On 30 November 1964 it was his 90th birthday.

WINSTON'S LOST DIARY
30 November 1964

Woken by somebody singing. It was Clemmie and the words were 'Happy Birthday to me.' 'That was lovely,' I told her.

A few cards and greetings arrived. I think the family counted 70,000 altogether. Didn't realize I knew so many people. Rested in the afternoon, listening to the old Harrow school songs.

Dinner with friends and the family – soup, oysters, partridge, ice cream and fruit – all washed down with the best champagne and wine. Everybody toasted my health and I managed to cut my cake. Not bad for a doddering old boy!

The light was fading fast. The playwright Noel Coward talked of Churchill in his last years wobbling around like a vast baby. 'He just lies in bed all day doing nothing,' said his old war comrade Montgomery, who came to try and cheer him up. His daughter Sarah remembered how he would ask her the time repeatedly. When she told him he would sigh deeply. Half an hour later he'd ask again, 'What is the time now?' 'Oh Lor!' he would say when she told him.

Once one of his grandchildren overheard the adults talking and excitedly ran in to see his grandad...

Winston's last public appearance was at the Other Club at the Savoy Hotel, where he sat in his usual place at the middle of the table with his back to the Thames. Only six weeks later he died – on Sunday, 24 January 1965. Seventy years before, on the same day, his father Lord Randolph had also died. Right to the end Winston kept his sense of history.

He would have been pleased to know that he joined his hero Nelson, the Duke of Wellington and William Gladstone as the only non-royals to be given the honour of a state funeral.

THE WINSTON WEEKLY
FAREWELL ISSUE
Sat 30 January 1965

NATION MOURNS 'OUR WINNIE'

The body of Winston Churchill was finally laid to rest with the sort of pomp and ceremony the great old man would have enjoyed. Churchill's only request was that there should be 'plenty of bands'. He got them – nine in all, as well as a whole lot more.

Over 300,000 people queued in the bitter cold to say goodbye as the coffin lay in Westminster Hall for three days and nights. Even Big Ben was silenced as the long procession moved to St Paul's. Churchill's body was then taken by boat up the River Thames, while a 19-gun salute was fired. Jets swooped overhead and the cranes on the Thames bowed like giants in salute.

Sir Winston was buried simply in Bladen churchyard alongside his parents and brother Jack. Westminster Abbey was offered but he didn't want to share it with 'so many people he did not like'.

As the train – a locomotive named *Battle of Britain* – carried Winston's coffin from London to Bladen, it passed a man standing on the flat roof of a house saluting in his old RAF uniform. For millions of ordinary men and women, Winston was the man who won the war and saved them from Hitler. Born the grandson of a duke, perhaps his greatest achievement was to become 'our Winnie'.